MW00459317

A Confirmation
of Faith

A Confirmation of Faith

Personal Reflections in Essays and Stories

STEPHEN ISAACSON

RESOURCE *Publications* · Eugene, Oregon

A CONFIRMATION OF FAITH
Personal Reflections in Essays and Stories

Resource Publications
An Imprint of Wipf and Stock Publishers
199 W. 8th Ave., Suite 3
Eugene, OR 97401

www.wipfandstock.com

PAPERBACK ISBN: 978-1-6667-8264-6
HARDCOVER ISBN: 978-1-6667-8265-3
EBOOK ISBN: 978-1-6667-8266-0

VERSION NUMBER 11/07/23

Contents

Preface

I CANNOT REMEMBER A time when I did not go to church. My very earliest memories include hearing Bible stories in Sunday school: Noah's Ark, Jonah in the whale, Joshua and the battle of Jericho, Jesus walking on the water, Christ being raised from the dead, and many others. My family attended an evangelical church, one that placed great emphasis on knowing Scripture, believing that, as the inspired word of God, "the Bible is without error in the original writings, the complete revelation of His will for salvation, and the ultimate authority by which every realm of human knowledge and endeavor should be judged."[1] My brothers and I were encouraged to memorize Scripture, and to take very seriously its teachings.

Our understanding was literal by default, having then little exposure to more nuanced translations, other interpretations and beliefs, and little life experience through which to evaluate our beliefs. I sat through hundreds of Sunday school classes and many sermons. At the age of thirteen, I was confirmed.

Confirmation is the sacrament in which a person makes a public confession and affirmation of their faith, usually in front of their faith community. Often this public affirmation represents the fulfillment of vows their parents and godparents made for them at their baptism (or dedication, in churches that do not practice infant baptism). In most liturgical traditions, the bishop lays his

---

1. Evangelical Free Church of America, "EFCA Statement of Faith," para. 2.

hands on those being confirmed and prays for the Holy Spirit to strengthen them.[2]

The term *catechesis* has been used from the first days of the early church for the preparation of new converts for their baptism and lifelong discipleship in the Christian faith. It is now most often used as preparation for confirmation of those who have already been baptized. The Rt. Rev. Steven Croft, Bishop of Oxford, maintains that the four Gospels were written as tools for catechesis.[3] The Gospel of Luke was specifically written to Theophilus "so that you may know the truth concerning the things about which you have been *catechized*" (Luke 1:4). *Catechesis* is a Greek term for instruction, literally meaning "to make resound, as with an echo."[4] In other words, it is instruction that resonates within us and is remembered again and again.

In my denomination, the Episcopal Church, the outline for this instruction (*catechism*) is presented in a question-answer format. It is not intended to be a complete statement of belief and practice. It provides a summary of the church's teaching, intended to serve as a point of departure for discussion by the catechist (lay or ordained teacher) with those who seek to understand the beliefs and practices of the Episcopal Church.[5]

The early church instituted an annual cycle of formation leading up to baptism at Easter. The instruction received from the beginning of the year would culminate in more intensive instruction during the forty days before Easter, the origin of Lent. The more structured format of catechesis, with a more formal arrangement of topics in a question-answer format, began sometime in the fourteenth century.[6] Catechism really took off during the Protestant Reformation with the conviction that catechesis was essential to the reform of the church.

2. Anglican Compass, "Anglican Glossary."

3. Croft, "Very Short History."

4. "Catechism," para. 3.

5. Armentrout and Slocum, *Episcopal Dictionary*, s.v. "Catechism."

6. "Brief History of Catechisms."

Confirmation may be the rite that takes place as a public Christian witness of our faith, but our convictions and sense of confirmed beliefs may change and expand as we also grow into our faith. As Richard Rohr has pointed out, most of us are never told that we can set out from the known and the familiar to take on a further journey.[7] He proposed that the purpose of the first half of life is to create a proper container for one's life and faith. However, the task of the second half of life is, quite simply, to find, reexamine, and sort the actual contents that this container was meant to hold in a way that may expand and refine our faith. The container is not an end in itself but exists for the sake of a deeper and fuller life.[8] Change and growth must become part of our relationship with God, and our life experiences lend deeper meaning to our faith.

As I said, my first catechesis experience was at age thirteen, attending weekly confirmation classes at the neighborhood Evangelical church my family attended. At our confirmation, we stood in white robes in front of the congregation on Sunday morning, with white carnations pinned to our collar, answering the pastor's questions about our faith and reciting together the Apostle's Creed. We each received a King James Bible with our name stamped in gold on the black leather cover.

As a young adult, various circumstances led me to question my commitment to my denomination. I was attending a small community church at the time that, on the surface, seemed to be grounded in sound evangelical teaching, but was managing to sap all the joy out of my Christian experience. I found it difficult to pray, and the religion I honored in church every Sunday morning was somewhat divorced from my life as I lived it during the week. I also came to know and respect other Christians in other cultures who had different faith practices and beliefs.

I became an Episcopalian at age thirty-five after attending an "Enquirer's Class" at St. Augustine's Church in Tempe, Arizona, while in graduate school. Father Frank sat down with the ten or twelve of us and opened the Book of Common Prayer to page

7. Rohr, *Falling Upward*, xvii.
8. Rohr, *Falling Upward*, 1.

845 ("An Outline of the Faith") where we took turns reading the question-answer pairs. After each recited answer, Father Frank would expound on the aspect of Christian doctrine addressed. It was a very traditional method of preparing catechumens, yet was instructive and interesting.

Years later, at Trinity Episcopal Cathedral in Portland, Oregon, I attended a very different kind of catechesis class, consisting of thoughtful and well-researched presentations, small group discussions, and interesting guest speakers. It didn't necessarily stick to the prayer book's catechism, but took us on a quick jaunt through the Old and New Testament, church history, and the components of the Eucharist among other things. It was in that class that I was introduced to Cornerstone, the intentional Benedictine community that would become a turning point in my spiritual life.

A few years later, I was asked by one of the Cathedral priests to be a catechesis mentor, meaning that I would see that participants had the materials they needed, look out for those who needed a little special attention, answer questions, facilitate discussions in one of the several small groups, and stand to support individual catechumens at their confirmation. I greatly enjoyed this role and did it for several years, each time learning something more about my faith and myself. In each of these catechesis experiences, I revisited and re-examined my faith, coming to new levels of understanding about spiritual practice and spiritual truths.

Over time, I expanded my ideas about God and learned new ways to study and interpret Scripture. I learned that the early church creeds evolved through a somewhat contentious process, and Christians have never all believed the same thing about almost everything, even concerning who Jesus was. The sacraments, especially baptism and communion, took on much deeper meaning for me. My concept and practice of prayer was greatly expanded to include listening, as well as talking, to God. I developed a new love for the Church.

You may think I am the last person who should write this book. I am not a theologian, pastor, or priest. I have never been to seminary or even taken a theology class. However, I have sat through many catechesis classes and thought deeply about my faith for many years. I've read many books by Christian authors I truly admire: C. S. Lewis, Thomas Merton, Esther DeWaal, Michael Casey, Richard Rohr, Cynthia Bourgeault, Barbara Brown Taylor, Marcus Borg, and Karen Armstrong, to name a few. I enjoy discussions about faith with my friends and members of a small group with whom I meet weekly.

This book is a result of my musings about the Christian faith over the years. It is not meant to be a substitute or a textbook for a catechesis class. The first thing the reader will notice is that it doesn't include every question-answer pair in the catechism. Rather, I've included a representative sampling of questions and answers that correspond to subjects I've written about and, I hope, cover some of the most essential topics in the catechism. They are personal and idiosynchratic responses to articles of faith—some in the form of essays, and some as stories—and are not meant to be taken too seriously as church teaching. You may agree or disagree with what I've said. However, I hope the discussion strikes a responsive chord and inspires thinking about your own faith experience.

Acknowledgements

As I was writing this book, I was lucky enough to have four good friends who welcomed—sometimes even demanded—my early drafts, and gave me long, thoughtful, and encouraging feedback. All four were people of faith, each having a different perspective on Christian teaching. Thank you, Laurie Eckman, Patricia Kessel, Roderick Thompson, and Ron Walker for your friendship, encouragement, and excellent advice. And, of course, thanks to Michael, who has never failed to encourage and support me. I am the luckiest of men.

Chapter 1

Q. *What do we learn about God as creator from the revelation to Israel?*

A. *We learn that there is one God, the Father Almighty, creator of heaven and earth, of all that is, seen and unseen.*

Q. *What does this mean?*

A. *This means that the universe is good, that it is the work of a single loving God who creates, sustains, and directs it. It means that the world belongs to its creator; and that we are called to enjoy it and to care for it in accordance with God's purposes. It means that all people are worthy of respect and honor, because all are created in the image of God, and all can respond to the love of God.*[1]

Who Is God?

1. Episcopal Church, *Book of Common Prayer*, 846.

"SCIENCE HAS PROVED THERE is no God!" declared my Uncle Norman, raising his voice. I'm not sure what I said that provoked his response. I may have made a passing reference to my church, and it annoyed him to no end that I was a person of faith.

I quietly replied, "So exactly how did science prove there is no God?" I was prepared to go into a discussion of epistemology, but Uncle Norman acknowledged my point, realizing the conversation had taken a wrong turn and hoping, I think, the discussion wouldn't go further into Christian apologetics.

He had reason to be angry at religion, growing up in a religious family with interpersonal dynamics right out of Eugene O'Neill. He had been preached at and brow-beaten his whole life. He had been dragged to church and heard lots about God. It just wasn't a God he had much use for.

I, too, had been raised in church, but had a different set of parents and a different way of coming to know God. I attended Sunday school and confirmation class and learned about God the way most of us learn about God—in church and from Scripture.

God as creator is the very first thing we learn about God. At the beginning of Genesis we learn that God created day and night, the waters covering the Earth, dry land and vegetation of every kind, the night sky that signals the seasons and days and years, swarms of living creatures in sea and air and land, and finally, "humankind in our image, according to our likeness" (Gen 1:26). And, at each stage of this holy evolution, looking at the unfolding creation, God saw that *it was good.*

But God didn't stop there. God continues to alter and expand creation. New mountains form. Islands can sink out of sight as sea levels rise and volcanic activity forms new ones in the archipelago. Rivers and streams change their courses, sometimes carving out valleys and canyons. Many species of creatures have become extinct as scientists discover that new life forms have evolved. Stars can become exploding supernovas that blast their parts into space, then disappear into black holes as new stars and planets are constantly being formed. Many of the great world religions picture the earth as being created and sustained by the steady breath of God.[2]

According to Tish Harrison Warren, Christians have a sacramental view of creation. As she puts it, "We believe that the stuff of earth carries within it the sacred presence of God."[3] Liberally paraphrasing the writing of Theophilus of Antioch, Olivier Clement wrote "God has given to the earth the breath that feeds it. God's breath vibrates in yours, in your voice. It is the breath of God that you breathe."[4]

We learn from the Hebrew Scriptures other things about God. On the one hand, God is a righteous judge (Ps 7:11) and, on the other hand, also merciful (Deut 4:31). God is our refuge and helper (Ps 46:1). God is love (1 John 4:8).

Hebrew Scriptures also make reference to the "spirit of the Lord" or "the divine spirit," suggesting other facets of God's being. The prophet Isaiah, in poetic language, also talks about a holy messenger who will come, "one who announces peace, who brings good news, who announces salvation" (Isa 52–53). This exalted servant, Isaiah prophesies, would astonish many but would also be "wounded for our transgressions, crushed for our iniquities." The Christian Testament authors interpreted these pronouncements as foreshadowing the crucified Messiah, the Christ.

Christian Scriptures (or New Testament) expand this understanding of God, referring to Jesus as the Son of God (Mark 1:11), the incarnate Logos (John 1:1–3), who was in the beginning with God and who, in fact, was/is God. In turn, Christ promised to send his Holy Spirit (John 14:26), our advocate, the "spirit of truth." Basil, bishop of Caesarea (ca. 330–79) developed the doctrine of the Trinity to show confused Christians at the time that Father, Son, and Holy Spirit were not three distinct gods.[5] But the word *Trinity*

---

2. Bourgeault, *Wisdom Jesus,* 162.

3. Warren, *Prayer in the Night,* 154.

4. Clement, *Roots of Mysticism,* 73.

5. Armstrong, *Case for God,* 114.

(*trias* in Greek) occurs much earlier, appearing first in the second-century writings of Theophilus of Antioch.[6]

I once heard a retired priest, in a Sunday morning forum, complain about the concept of the Trinity: one God in three persons. He just couldn't wrap his head around it. When Trinity Sunday came around every year, he would always find someone else to preach, because he had no idea what to say.

However, believers worldwide have known God as a heavenly parent and God incarnate as an obedient son who, as it happened, was also God (John 1:1). We also know God as an ever-present Spirit "who rides on a gentle breeze, who strengthens our bindings, and who offers hope eternal."[7] Augustine of Hippo wrote that, if we looked within, we would discover a triad in our own minds in the faculties of memory (*memoria*), understanding (*intellectus*), and will or love (*voluntas*) that give us an insight into the triune nature of God.[8]

I have always accepted the notion of the Trinity, while also thinking of it as one of those mysteries of our faith that I may never completely understand. Trying to find a personal analogy, I've thought about my brother, Jim. To me, he was the annoying little brother that I got into frequent arguments with as we were growing up. That is, until the year we were both students at the University of Washington and I witnessed another student say something completely insensitive to him in the Student Union that raised my protective hackles. I realized then just how much it meant to me to have a brother.

To my parents, Jim was a son. My dad called him "Jimbo." He was a small but very smart kid who was often teased for looking much younger than he was. My parents' concern for his physical and emotional development gave way to extreme pride when, as a young adult, he was called to ordained ministry.

To my nephews and niece, Jim is a very loving father who craves time with each of his children and is ferociously proud of

6. "Theophilus of Antioch."

7. United Society, "Shore to Shore," 122.

8. Armstrong, *Case for God*, 120.

the adults they have become. In other words, Jim had three different facets to his person, and these three different roles were all part
of the same wonderful being.

However, I realize this is an imperfect analogy, because Jim is
not three different persons who happen to be one being. The crucial yet paradoxical thing in traditional Trinitarian theology is the
true and real distinction between the three persons (*hypostases*)
while retaining the unity of substance (*ousia*), the oneness of God.
The Son of God suffered in his body on the cross; God the Father
did not. Jesus prayed to the Father (i.e., not himself). After Jesus
tells his disciples that he will go away and prepare a place for them,
he promises that the Father will send "another Advocate" that will
be with them forever (John 14:16).[9] Yet all three are part of one
divine being. (Jesus said to Philip, "Whoever has seen me has seen
the Father"; John 14:9.)

Our liturgical tradition makes frequent reference to the first
person of the Trinity as "God the Father," and I was once told
that people—men especially—tend to think of God in the same
way they think about their earthly father. My dad was a patient,
good-natured, if occasionally emotionally distant man, and I think
that's how I've always imagined God. Of course, this theory would
present significant challenges to the faith of those who had absent,
demanding, or abusive fathers.

Stanford research psychologists found that people are constantly exposed to the image of God as a white male (although
6 percent of downloaded God images were of actor Morgan
Freeman).[10] In a series of subsequent studies, participants reported that God was more male than female. They also found
that white Christians were more likely to say God was white, and
black Christians more likely to say God was black. (These findings
corresponded to who participants thought should become leaders.) Evidence exists, therefore, that to a large degree, rightly or
wrongly, we all create our own concept of God.

9. Thanks to the Rev. Roderick Thompson for this insight.
10. De Witt, "Who People Believe."

Laura Swan reminds us that our images of God are images; they are not, in themselves, who God is.[11] To underscore that very point, Diana Eck retells the story of the Hindu god Krishna who beckons milkmaids to the forest to dance in the middle of the night.[12] Krishna magically multiples himself to dance simultaneously with each one of them. The moment that a milkmaid became possessive, thinking that the god was dancing with her alone, Krishna disappeared. Eck concludes by saying that the moment we human beings grasp God with jealousy and possessiveness, we may very well lose hold of God. As Gregory Boyle puts it, "God can get tiny if we're not careful."[13]

When Moses asked God on Mount Sinai what name for God he should give to the people, the answer was "I AM WHO I AM." In other words, God would not be put into a box. N. T. Wright compared speaking about God to staring into the sun. It's too dazzling to perceive clearly. He continued, "It's easier, actually, to look away from the sun itself and to enjoy the fact that, once it's well and truly risen, you can see everything else clearly."[14] The enormous, dazzling, unfathomable nature of God makes it difficult to completely understand or describe the Divine. Greek Orthodox theologians were right in saying that any statement about God should have two qualities: it must be *paradoxical*, to remind us that the divine cannot fit into our limited human categories, and *apophatic*, leading us to speechless awe.[15] The important point is this: that speechless awe comes not just from a factual knowledge of what the Scriptures say about God or an intellectual understanding of qualities attributed to God by early theologians. The deep appreciation of the unfathomable comes from an experiential faith. It is not enough to know of God as creator without also having felt the steady breath of God in one's own life. One cannot fully understand God's mercy without having asked for and received God's

11. Swan, *Engaging Benedict*, 44.

12. Eck, *Encountering God*, 46–47.

13. Boyle, *Tattoos on the Heart*, 19.

14. Wright, "God," 291.

15. Armstrong, *Great Transformation*, 393.

forgiveness. Appreciating God's love comes from the experience of being upheld in divine love even as one is going through life's most difficult moments. This is the familiarity with God that is most important to have.

Chapter 2

Q. What are we by nature?

A. We are part of God's creation, made in the image of God.

Q. What does it mean to be created in the image of God?

A. It means that we are free to make choices: to love, to create, to reason, and to live in harmony with creation and with God.

What Are We?

MY DAILY ROUTINE GOES something like this. I wake up as light begins to fill the bedroom. I pull on my sweats and slippers and go downstairs to turn up the furnace and make coffee. As I'm preparing my oatmeal, our dog Zaki will usually rouse and want to go outside. After that's done, I'll read the paper as I'm downing my bowl of cereal. I spend some time in prayer (usually the office of Morning Prayer). Then I exercise for about twenty minutes. After showering, I answer emails and do some reading. After lunch I walk the dog. When I return I grab a book and read until I dose off. After I rouse from my nap I'll try to do some work, practice the piano, then watch the news until dinner. After dinner, I usually do some writing and then go downstairs to watch TV with Mike before bedtime. On some days I manage to squeeze in coffee or a meal with a friend or two.

Here's the thing: I can go a whole day—a whole week—without thinking about who I am, the things my body can do with little effort, the miracle of cognitive abilities that allow me to read and write, the degree to which music is such a gratifying part of my life, and the fact that I've sustained a pretty nice relationship with a wonderful man for many years now. I don't give a lot of thought to what it means to be human. I just am, I guess.

What are we? To begin with, human beings are remarkable creations with remarkable bodies that have been given the ability to mostly manage millions of sensations and signals that penetrate our senses every second. Saint Augustine wrote,

> You, Lord my God, are the giver of life and a body to a baby. As we see, you have endowed it with senses. You have coordinated the limbs. You have adorned it with a beautiful form, and for the coherence and preservation of the whole you have implanted all the instincts of a living being.[1]

David Brooks says that we are like "spiritual Grand Central stations."[2] We are social beings that want to reach out and connect. We seek, more than anything else, to establish deeper and more complete connections. Our unconscious wants to achieve communion with work, family, friends, community, and cause. We long for love. We long for God. As Saint Augustine wrote, "You have made us for yourself, O Lord, and our heart is restless until it rests in you."[3] Since humankind is made in the Creator's image and likeness, creativity must be an essential characteristic of our nature. There is an abundance of evidence that this is so. God created the day and the night, and humans developed the calendar and the

---

1. Augustine of Hippo, *Conf.* 1.7 (p. 12).

2. Brooks, *Social Animal*, xvii.

3. Augustine, *Conf.* 1.1 (p. 1).

clock to keep track of times and seasons. God separated the waters and created land, and humans invented the sextant and compass to navigate and explore lands and oceans. Humankind went on to create the waterwheel, concrete, the printing press, vaccines, steam engines, batteries, transistors, and microchips, to name just a few.

But creativity does not just exist in remarkable invention. It blesses our lives in many ways. I walk down Bridgeton Road, a small one-mile street near my home that runs along the South Channel of the Columbia River. It overlooks boat moorages and floating home communities. I always stop to look at a simple rectangular house with sign over the front door that reads "Papa's Garden." For several years, it has been the home of an immigrant family, and every square foot of its tiny front yard is filled with dozens and dozens of flowering plants: geraniums and peonies, but mostly roses. "Papa" died five years ago, but his daughter faithfully keeps up the garden. The profusion of vibrant color surrounding the house is a gift to the street and all who pass by.

A little farther down Bridgeton Road, I come to another very humble house, in need of paint and other repairs. Barry lives there, and from the elaborately decorated fence in front of the house, he is clearly a divinely inspired artist. The border with the street is a fascinating collection of plumes, dried flowers, statuary, plastic flamingos, glass beads, a painting or two, seashells, clusters of plastic grapes, and interesting found objects. It is an artfully arranged collection, and a walker's eye is drawn to it, no matter how often they've passed by.

One can see other signs of human creativity everywhere. Every week Dorothy, a delightful woman who works for Trinity Cathedral's food ministries, checks what the cathedral might have in its pantry and walk-in cooler, as well as what the gleaners bring in from local businesses, and puts together, with her kitchen team, tasty and nutritious meals for the unhoused and food insecure neighbors who come to our door. Many say it's the best meal in town.

Humans created written language and music and ways to clothe themselves and artistic expressions of every kind, as they continue to do. Gabriel Fauré began work on his moving Requiem in D minor about the time of both his father's and mother's death, but he insisted they were not the motivation for the work. He told an interviewer, "As to my Requiem, perhaps I have also instinctively sought to escape from what is thought right and proper. After all the years of accompanying burial services on the organ I know it all by heart. I wanted to write something different."[4]

Danish architect Jørn Utzon changed the course of twentieth-century architecture in his design of the Sydney Opera House, Australia's most famous tourist attraction. Frank Gehry said of the structure that it was a building "well ahead of its time, far ahead of available technology . . . a building that changed the image of an entire country."[5]

Creativity is a fundamental activity of human information processing. It is grounded in ordinary mental processes. Cognitive neuroscientists have found that discrete neural circuits that process information in noncreative ways are the same neural circuits that generate creative or novel combinations of that information.[6] In other words, every human, as created by God, is wired for creativity.

In almost every aspect of life, from feeding a child to planting a garden to solving a business problem, creativity plays an exceedingly crucial role. Creative insights can occur either spontaneously or as a result of methodical deliberation.[7] Creative processes also can occur in either the emotional or cognitive structures of the brain.

Creativity comes into play in our spiritual lives as well. In past centuries, music and art were created for the glory of God.[8] Artists had a consciousness that their own creativity was a divine gift, an opening for God to work through them. However, artists aren't

---

4. Orledge, *Gabriel Fauré*, 115.

5. Hawthorne, "Jorn Utzon Dies at 90," para. 17.

6. Dietrich, "Cognitive Neuroscience."

7. Dietrich, "Cognitive Neuroscience."

8. Cameron, *Walking in This World*.

the only ones who have a part in revealing God in the world. As Barbara Brown Taylor puts it:

> God has no hands but ours, no bread but the bread we bake, no prayers but the ones we make, whether we know what we're doing or not. When Christians speak of the mystery of the incarnation, this is what they mean: for reasons beyond anyone's understanding, God has decided to be made known in flesh.[9]

This is not to say that all of our efforts are successful. Millions have failed. Mistakes are part of everyone's learning. We are imperfect beings. Thousands of doctors, psychologists, sociologists, and self-help gurus write books for readers who are hoping to attain better lives by achieving clearer thinking, better skills, healthier habits, or more fulfilling relationships. The 2020–22 pandemic years showed us that humans don't always handle stress very well. The news was full of people who attacked health care workers, screamed at waiters, threw tantrums in stores, abused their spouses, and threw punches at flight attendants.

As the writers of the Catechism in the *Book of Common Prayer* assert, "human beings have misused their freedom and made wrong choices." If, as Saint Augustine maintained, there is something in our being that longs for and seeks union with God, so too it seems, is a restless spirit that resists God's influence in our lives. The Catechism goes on to say that we've rebelled against God, and we put ourselves in the place of God. In my spiritual struggles I often think of the words from this old hymn: "Prone to wander, Lord I feel it, prone to leave the God I love."[10]

However, for better or for worse, we are cocreators with God of our lives, cooperating and collaborating in new ways of thinking and being. The writer of the epistle to the Ephesians says, "You were taught to put away your former way of life, your old self, corrupt and deluded by its lusts, and to be renewed in the spirit of your minds, and to clothe yourselves with the new self, created

9. Taylor, *Altar in the World*, 201.

10. "Come Thou Fount of Every Blessing." Words by Robert Robinson (1735–90).

according to the likeness of God in true righteousness and holiness" (Eph 4:22–24). Paul writes, "Do not be conformed to this world, but be transformed by the renewing of your minds, so that you may discern what is the will of God—what is good and acceptable and perfect" (Rom 2:12).

Our imperfect relationship with God is coupled with an imperfect self-knowledge, at least in this life. The epistle writer Paul wrote, "For now we see in a mirror, dimly, but then we will see face to face. Now I know only in part; then I will know fully, even as I have been fully known" (1 Cor 13:12).

Chapter 3

Q. *Why do we live apart from God and out of harmony with creation?*

A. *From the beginning, human beings have misused their freedom and made wrong choices.*

Q. *What is sin?*

A. *Sin is the seeking of our own will instead of the will of God, thus distorting our relationship with God, with other people, and with all creation.*

The Uncomfortable Reality of Sin

SIN IS NOT MY favorite topic, and it seems to be an uncomfortable subject for many mainstream Christians to talk about. In searching the indexes of several Christian books, sin isn't even referenced.

The other night, I posted this on Facebook: "I'm having a little trouble with a piece I'm writing, and you could help. Finish this sentence: The thing about sin is . . ." I received thirty-eight responses.

Some thought of sin as something trite that we should brush off. "Banal," was one person's response. "It doesn't really exist," said another. A couple of FB friends wrote about it as inevitable. Some wrote about it as a distraction. "Just a stepping off the path," one wrote. "It distracts us from faithful living," wrote another.

Others wrote about its effect, especially on one's own psyche. "There are earthly consequences humans endure," said one, and two friends offered that the natural consequence is "getting lost." Another defined it as "a kind of blindness." A retired therapist wrote that the thing about sin is "our own guilt and self-focused vision." "It is never silent," said another. My friend Greg wrote, "It's hard to not beat yourself up and hard to get that it's not a moral judgment as much as it is acknowledging you have separated yourself from your sacredness."

Some reflected on how God sees it. "As soon as we are conscious of it, it is forgiven," said my priest friend, Julia. Mary, a very wise Christian educator friend, wrote, "We were all made for goodness in God's very image and since God is Love, sin does not separate God from us, but it does separate us from one another and from ourselves and from a full sense of knowing that we are loved by God." Several stated that it doesn't change how much God loves us.

Another priest friend questioned whether any discussion of sin is complete without some mention of repentance. Is God's forgiveness of sin true for those who are conscious of sin and yet impenitent? The importance of repentance is mentioned in the Catechism's discussion of both Baptism and the Eucharist. Facebook friend Chris pointed out that "we are so quick to see it in others, but not so quick to see it in ourselves."

Then there is the enticing aspect of sin. Mark Twain wrote, "There is a charm about the forbidden that makes it unspeakably desirable." And Oscar Wilde famously quipped, "I can resist everything except temptation."

Subjectively, one's concept of sin changes as one matures and rubs up against life as most people experience it. One of my very first memories as a toddler is reaching through the picket fence in my yard to grab and claim the toy truck laying in the grass on the other side of the fence (not understanding then the impossibility of bringing the truck through the slats of the fence). I was told that, no, I could not have that truck because it belonged to someone else, one of my first lessons in learning what was wrong to do.

As a child, sins were the bad things that one shouldn't do. Early on they included disobeying, lying, saying bad words, and hitting my brothers. In my religious tradition they went on to include taking the Lord's name in vain, dancing, drinking alcohol, and smoking. Going to movies wasn't technically a sin, but certainly a gray area—not something a Christian should do, given the loose lifestyles portrayed in many films. Once when I came home from our neighborhood grocery store, my mother chastised me for sucking on a candy cigarette. "Abstain from all *appearance* of evil," she instructed me from Scripture.

While the topic of sin is sidestepped by some Christian authors, it seems to be fruitful territory for others. Looking online, I was amazed at the many and varied ways in which sin has been parsed and disaggregated. Roman Catholic teaching makes the distinction between mortal and venial sins. One also can sort offenses in terms of sins against God, sins against others, and sins against oneself.[1] Then there are offenses against individuals as compared to those against groups. One could also differentiate between the moral wrong that has been done by an act of sin (sometimes called "the problem of past sin"), and the moral wrong one is likely to do (sometimes called "the problem of future sin"). Sin can be an action (broadly construed to include omissions as well as commissions), a state (the incapacity to do or to be anything worthy of God), or a disposition (disorder in which our affections are skewed, directed to the wrong objects). *Yikes!* I think. *If I manage to avoid one of those, I'm certain to be caught in another.* One

---

1. Timpe, "Sin in Christian Thought."

Facebook friend pointed out how ubiquitous it seems, especially when considering "things done and left undone."

Augustine of Hippo formulated the doctrine of Original Sin, the evil inherent in every human being that was passed down from Adam.[2] This doctrine became popular among Protestant reformers. According to Karen Armstrong, Jewish exegetes never saw the sin of Adam in that catastrophic light, and the Greek Christians have never accepted the doctrine of Original Sin.[3] Timpe states that the doctrine of original sin cannot be found in the Bible, although verses like this raise a question in my mind: "Therefore, just as sin came into the world through one man, and death came through sin, and so death spread to all because all have sinned" (Rom 5:12). Gregory the Great labeled certain offenses against God as the "seven deadly sins": gluttony, lust, avarice, anger, sadness, acedia (sloth), and vainglory.[4] In a 1925 sermon in Westminster Abbey, Frederick Lewis Donaldson added corporate, societal sins, which he defined as the "seven social sins": wealth without work, pleasure without conscience, knowledge without character, commerce without morality, science without humanity, worship without sacrifice, and politics without principle.

No one in my Facebook survey mentioned the Ten Commandments, although certainly they have imprinted themselves on our collective unconscious as a definitive list of sins. And then the book of Leviticus goes on to enumerate many acts that are forbidden, some being labeled abominations. Karen Armstrong tells the famous Talmudic story of Rabbi Hillel who was one day approached by a pagan.[5] The man promised to convert to Judaism if Hillel could teach him the entire Torah standing on one leg. Hillel lifted one foot and replied, "What is hateful to yourself, do not to your fellow man. That is the whole of the Torah and the remainder is but commentary." In other words, Rabbi Hillel had formulated a Jewish version of the Golden Rule, implying that the

2. Timpe, "Sin in Christian Thought."

3. Armstrong, *Case for God*, 122.

4. Casey, *Grace*, 57.

5. Armstrong, *Case for God*, 79.

essence of Jewish teaching was the refusal to inflict pain on other human beings.

Christians will immediately call to mind Jesus's answer to the scribe who asked him, "Which commandment is the first of all?" Jesus answered, "The first is, 'Hear, O Israel: the Lord our God, the Lord is one; you shall love the Lord your God with all your heart, and with all your soul, and with all your mind, and with all your strength.' The second is this, 'You shall love your neighbor as yourself'" (Mark 12:28–31). Matthew adds to this account these final words: "On these two commandments hang all the law and the prophets" (Matt 22:40). In other words, in God's eyes sin is trumped by love.

A few years ago, I attended a memorial service for a family member in another state. After several people had spoken about the one who had died, one family member took over the podium to say what was on his heart. After talking about the years he had wandered away from the Lord, he launched into the topic of sin, reaching an emotional climax with the words, "If you're living in sin, you're living under God's wrath."

There were so many things wrong with that pronouncement that I scarcely knew where to begin. It bothered me for days. The truth is we all live with sin. It's part of our life and struggle every day. In a letter from Martin Luther to Philip Melanchthon, written while hiding out to avoid execution, he wrote,

> If you are a preacher of mercy, do not preach an imaginary but the true mercy. If the mercy is true, you must therefore bear the true, not an imaginary sin. God does not save those who are only imaginary sinners. Be a sinner, and let your sins be strong, but let your trust in Christ be stronger, and rejoice in Christ who is the victor over sin, death, and the world. We will commit sins while we are here, for this life is not a place where justice resides. We, however, says Peter (2 Peter 3:13), are looking forward to a new heaven and a new earth where justice will reign. It suffices that through God's glory we have recognized the Lamb who takes away the sin of the

18

world. No sin can separate us from Him, even if we were to kill or commit adultery thousands of times each day.[6]

However, the epistler to the Romans would caution us: "Should we continue in sin in order that grace may abound? By no means! How can we who died to sin go on living in it?" (Rom 6:1–2).

In his wonderful book on grace, Michael Casey explained that resident vices exist in every human soul, tendencies that lead us away from God and, more importantly, cause us to become discouraged and to lose faith in the possibility of attaining close friendship with God.[7]

He goes on to say, "Perhaps it is true . . . that we will not experience the ministry of angels until we have consented to confront the wild beasts within us; only then will we hear the divine response, 'My grace is enough for you: power is made perfect in weakness' (2 Cor 12:9)."[8]

6. Reeves, "Did Luther Tell Us," para. 7.

7. Casey, *Grace*, 56.

8. Casey, *Grace*, 57.

Chapter 4

Q. *What is the nature of God revealed in Jesus?*
A. *God is love.*

God in the Flesh

I CANNOT REMEMBER A time when I did not hear about Jesus, and my earliest awareness of him was associated with love. My first Sunday school song was probably "Jesus loves me, this I know . . ." Or was it "Jesus loves the little children, all the children of the world"? I was taught to pray to this kind, loving Jesus. But that Jesus was a divine superhero, not a real flesh-and-blood person like me who was sometimes upset, sometimes anxious, sometimes silly. Often the Jesus stories were taught using a flannelgraph, cut-out paper figures of Bible characters that were moved about on an easel board covered in flannel material. As I remember, they were the gentle stories: Christ the good shepherd, the healer who made the blind man see, the preacher who magically turned five loaves and two fishes into a meal for thousands. The stories of his radical defiance were saved for much later: telling religious leaders they were whitewashed tombstones, overturning money tables in the temple, cursing the fig tree that had no fruit.

On one of their wanderings, Jesus asked his disciples, "Who do people say that the Son of Man is?" And they answered, "Some say John the Baptist, but others Elijah, and still others Jeremiah or one of the prophets." And he followed up with, "But who do you say that I am?" Simon Peter answered, "You are the Messiah, the Son of the living God" (Matt 16:13–16).

Not everyone then, nor does everyone now, agree who Jesus really was. He was given many titles: Lamb of God, Rabbi (teacher), King of the Jews, Messiah, Master, and Son of God among them, although Jesus most often referred to himself as the Son of Man. The extraordinary influence of his life and teaching is evident in the fact that it was incorporated into the Gospels produced a generation after his death and took fire in cosmopolitan places like Antioch, Damascus, and Rome.[1]

As Reza Aslan explains it, the problem with establishing the historical Jesus is that, outside of the New Testament, there is little historical record of the man who would so permanently alter the course of human history.[2] The earliest nonbiblical reference to Jesus comes from Flavius Josephus, a first-century Jewish historian, who fleetingly refers to "James, the brother of Jesus, the one they call messiah." Second-century historians like Tacitus and Pliny the Younger also mention Jesus of Nazareth but reveal little about him, except for his arrest and execution. These accounts shed little light on the details of Jesus's life. Although we know practically nothing about his childhood and adolescence, many assume that, as a young man, he trained as a carpenter working with Joseph. Scriptural accounts indicate that Jesus had brothers and sisters. Details from Jesus's teaching suggest it was a poor home: details such as sewing on a new patch, putting new wine in old wineskins, using only a little leaven.[3]

Marcus Borg makes a distinction between the "pre-Easter" and "post-Easter" Jesus, the pre-Easter Jesus as the historical figure up to the time of his death, and the post-Easter Jesus being the Christ of Christian tradition and experience, as informed by the

1. Chilton, *Pure Kingdom*, 47.

2. Aslan, *Zealot*, xxiv–xxv.

3. LaSor, *Men Who Knew Christ*, 16–17.

accounts in the New Testament.[4] Among the historically verifiable facts about Jesus, Borg includes:

- He was a healer. More healing stories are told about Jesus than about anybody else in Jewish tradition, and he attracted a large following.

- He was a teacher with a remarkable use of language, often metaphorical, poetic, and imaginative, as expressed in short sayings and compelling short stories.

- He did things other religious figures would not dare do: He ate meals with those others would not touch or approach. He carried out radical demonstrations such as overturning the tables of money changers and driving out sellers from the temple.[5]

The timing of Jesus's coming to earth was significant. As the Bible expresses it, he appeared "when the fullness of time was come" (Gal 4:4). He came to a tiny nation, on a popular trade route, within a world empire controlled by a standing army of a quarter-million men.[6] The people of that occupied nation were under severe oppression and were anxiously looking for a leader, a Messiah.

The understanding of the post-Resurrection Christ came into being through the extensive letters written by the apostle Paul to the budding Christian communities in various parts of the Roman empire and the Gospels written after them, stories and teachings remembered by Jesus's disciples. Among the many New Testament stories, these images are among the most salient:

In a small town, in an animal shed, a young woman who cannot find other shelter gives birth in the straw to a tiny infant. The new husband provides whatever help he can as the newborn is cleaned and wrapped and placed in a feeding trough to sleep. A

---

4. Borg, *Meeting Jesus*, 15–16.

5. Borg, *Meeting Jesus*, 30–31.

6. LaSor, *Men Who Knew Christ*, 1–4.

few shepherds look in to see what is happening. They say angels told them to come.

At eight days old the infant is brought to the temple to be circumcised, as was the Jewish custom. When Simeon, the priest, takes the child in his arms, he is suddenly very moved and praises God, saying, "My eyes have seen the Savior whom you have prepared for all the world to see."

At about age twelve or thirteen, the child's parents bring him to the temple in Jerusalem for his *bar mitzvah*. During the return to their village, they realize he is not among the travelers. Hurrying back to the temple, they find him in deep discussion with the priests, who marvel at his understanding.

Years later, at about age thirty, Jesus comes to a desert stream to be baptized by his cousin, a popular vagabond prophet. When the prophet (John) sees him, he tells his followers, "Here is the Lamb of God who takes away the sin of the world!" As Jesus comes up from the water after his baptism, he sees heaven being torn open and "the Spirit descending on him like a dove" (Mark 1:10).

During his relatively short life, Jesus taught about love. For example, early in his ministry, Jesus noticed a large crowd that had followed him up a mountain side, and he addressed them in a rather long sermon, at the end of which he focused on the subject of love. He said, "You have heard that it was said, 'You shall love your neighbor and hate your enemy.' But I say to you, Love your enemies and pray for those who persecute you, so that you may be children of your Father in heaven" (Matt 5:43–45). At another time, he told his followers, "You should love your neighbor as yourself" (Matt 19:19).

Jesus taught the importance of love in the short stories (parables) he told his followers. One parable was about a King, sitting on his throne, separating all the peoples of the earth, like a shepherd separating sheep from goats, putting the "sheep" on his right hand and the "goats" on his left. The king said to those on his right, "Come, you that are blessed, inherit the kingdom prepared for you. I was hungry and you gave me food, I was thirsty and you gave me something to drink, I was a stranger and you welcomed me, I was naked and you gave me clothing, I was sick and you took care of me, I was in prison and you visited me." These righteous individuals answered, "Lord, when did we ever see you hungry and give you food, or something to drink? And when did we see you alone or give you clothing or visit you in prison?" And the king answered them, "Truly, every time you did it to the least of my brothers and sisters, you did it to me." Then he turned to those at his left hand and cursed those who gave him no food or drink, did not welcome him or clothe him, did not visit him when sick or in prison, saying "Just as you did not do it to one of my poor brothers and sisters, you did not do it to me" (Matt 25:31–46).

He taught about a shepherd who, having a hundred sheep, lost one of them, and left the other ninety-nine and went after the one that is lost until he found it (Luke 15:4–7). He taught about a man who lovingly welcomed back his son who left home and squandered his money in dissolute living (Luke 15:11–27). Jesus illustrated what he meant when he said "Love your neighbor as yourself" with the story of a traveling Samaritan, an outcast, people the Jews despised for intermarrying with non-Jews. The Samaritan sees the victim of crime, lying at the side of the road, half dead. He was moved with pity and provided him first aid, bandaging his wounds and putting him on his mule. He brought him to an inn, and took care of him there, paying the innkeeper to look after him when he had to leave (Luke 10:27–37). To summarize, Jesus defined love in terms of compassion to those who are lost, hungry, poor, sick, imprisoned, or victimized. Love for one's neighbor included strangers in need—even enemies.

At that final meal with his disciples, he had one last message for them about love: "Just as I have loved you, you also should love one another. By this everyone will know that you are my disciples, if you have love for one another" (John 13:34–35).

Jesus also taught by example. One has to wonder about the kind of magnetism and love Jesus demonstrated to those he met to compel four fisherman (first Simon and Andrew, then James and John) to leave their boats and nets and follow him. They, as well as other followers, witnessed remarkable acts of compassion.

One day, Jesus was moved with pity when a leper came to him, asking to be healed. Jesus did the unthinkable: he touched him, covered as he was with ulcers and lesions, and the man was healed. In Samaria, Jesus had a heart-to-heart, but eyebrow-raising, talk with a woman drawing water at the village well at noon to avoid those who would scorn her. (Respectable women drew water in the morning or evening, cooler times of the day.) Jesus even loved tax collectors, whom everyone else despised, calling one (Levi) to join his band of disciples, and inviting himself to dinner with another (Zacchaeus) whom he spotted in a tree.

This extraordinary love was shown in the patience he showed to his disciples, the delight he had in the little children who were brought to him, and the love he showed Martha and Mary, grieving with them at their brother Lazarus's death. When the rich young man asked him what he must do to inherit eternal life, and Jesus told him, "Go, sell what you own, and give the money to the poor, . . . then come, follow me," Mark's Gospel also adds that Jesus, "looking at him, loved him" (Mark 10:21), knowing the young man would turn away. John's Gospel tells us that Jesus, knowing that his hour had come to depart from this world, "loved his own who were in the world, he loved them to the end" (John 13:1).

Huston Smith divides the Jewish people in Jesus's time into four main groups: the Sadducees, the Essenes, the Pharisees, and the Zealots. In spite of the many confrontations Jesus had with Pharisees, this was the group with which he was most closely aligned and their emphasis on holiness.[7] The interpretation of the holiness code that Jesus found unacceptable—and spoke out against—were the lines this code drew between people. It was not just that certain acts or certain objects were deemed clean or unclean (food and its preparation, for example), but the code went on to categorize people as clean or unclean, pure or defiled, based on their ability to practice the demanding code. Jesus recognized a destructive social structure with barriers between people who were clean and unclean, Jew and gentile, righteous and sinner. Any number of people fell through these cracks to become the lost, the

7. Smith, *Soul of Christianity*, 43.

rejected, the outcast, and the forsaken.[8] It was to those marginalized ones that he reached out.

However, as important as Jesus's example and teaching was to the Christian message, his most important role was that of *savior*. The baptismal rite includes this question to the candidate: "Do you turn to Jesus Christ and accept him as your Savior?" The Nicene Creed we recite each Sunday reminds us that "For us and for our salvation he came down from heaven." And the Christian Testament makes many references to "the Savior of the world," "our God and Savior," and "our Lord and Savior Jesus Christ," among others. The exact meaning of Christ's death and its relationship to our sin and the sins of the world is a subject of some debate.[9] However, Scripture seems clear on the point that Jesus as God incarnate offered himself to save us from sin and its consequences and bring us to eternal life with him. God's incarnation in the person of Jesus and his sacrificial death revealed God's love for creation. The solution to the enigma of an enormous, dazzling, unfathomable God was that God reached out to humankind in human form in a way that made God more relatable and, thereby, a relationship to God more accessible. Albert Schweitzer addressed the puzzle of the historical Jesus this way:

> He comes to us as One unknown, without a name, as of old, by the lakeside, He came to those men who knew Him not. He speaks to us the same word: "Follow thou me!" and sets us to the tasks which He has to fulfil for our time. He commands. And to those who obey Him, whether they be wise or simple, He will reveal Himself in the toils, the conflicts, the sufferings which they shall pass through in His fellowship, and, as an ineffable mystery, they shall learn in their own experience Who He is.[10]

Christianity is unique among religions in the relational way it conjoins the divine and the human. As Huston Smith put it,

8. Smith, *Soul of Christianity*, 44–45.

9. See chapter 6 for a further discussion of Christ's atonement.

10. Schweitzer, *Quest of the Historical Jesus*, 561.

"A bridge must touch both banks, and Christ was the bridge that joined humanity to God."[11] It remains with us to meet Christ on that bridge, let him envelope us in his love, and follow his steps to a path that leads to eternal life.

11. Smith, *Soul of Christianity*, 102.

Chapter 5

Q. *What is the New Commandment?*

A. *The New Commandment is that we love one another as Christ loved us.*

Loving Lillian

ONE SUNDAY MORNING, THE dean of the cathedral I attend invited parishioners to come have lunch on Wednesdays with the church's low-income neighbors who came every week to be fed a hot meal. I was shamefully aware that these were people I usually made a point of avoiding in my day-to-day life, but I summoned up the courage and came to have lunch, sitting with a group of men with whom I managed to strike up a very pleasant conversation. It was at this meal that I decided to come back the following week to be a lunch volunteer.

I gradually came to know a very colorful cast of characters that came each week to the Wednesday lunch: a combination of homeless street people, residents of three low-income high-rises in the neighborhood, and others who were down on their luck. Typically they found, after paying their rent and electrical bills and, for many, prescriptions, that they had very little money left over for food. "Food insecure" is what the social services people called them.

One of the first lunch guests I got to know was Lillian.[1] I guessed her age to be seventy-ish. She had a wiry build and her back was knobby and bent from scoliosis. She had an interesting taste in clothes, tending toward fabrics with animal prints or Disney cartoon characters, and her loose pajama-type pants tending not to coordinate well with blouses that covered her large breasts hanging down to her waist. Her tightly curled hair was always in place and she wore just a touch of makeup.

She walked into the parish hall where we served the lunch like she owned the place and found a seat at a table after stopping to say a few words to two or three people she knew. She had a flirtatious sparkle in her eye when she smiled at you. If she wanted something, she'd let you know, shouting from her seat, "Hey, good lookin', what do you have to do to get a cup of coffee around here?" or "Hey boobie, would you come over here for a minute please." She had the gravelly baritone voice of a woman who had smoked all her life.

One day I happened to be walking by the door as she was entering the parish hall and she grabbed my arm. "Hey, good lookin', I saw your picture out there." She dragged me to the foyer where, sure enough, my photo was posted along with other Vestry members on the bulletin board. She was proud of herself for having spotted me. "You're the best lookin' man in the whole bunch, yes you are."

That was the start of a friendship like no other I've ever had. Lillian would seek me out every time she came, pulling my arm close against her sagging breast to share some confidence or observation with me. She ate slowly, because she had no teeth, and occasionally had me take a plate of food away because it was too hard or crusty for her to chew. She flirted shamelessly with Jack, an older gay man in his mid-seventies who, with his sidekick Jerry, managed the hot beverage cart, giving out coffee, tea, or hot chocolate to the guests. And before she left the hall after eating,

---

1. This is a true story, but I've changed a few names to protect identities.

she made the rounds, saying good-bye to Heidi, the cook, Fred, the doorman, and anyone else she happened to know.

One day, as she was leaving, she pulled me close to her and asked, confidentially, what she should do if she wanted to come to church some Sunday. I told her that our service was at ten o'clock and she would be very welcome. She still seemed a little hesitant.

"Would you like to sit with me on Sunday?" I asked. She lit up at that idea. "Meet me right out here on the breezeway at quarter to 10," I continued, "and we can go in together."

On Sunday morning, I found her waiting for me on the breezeway before the service, wearing a tiger print blouse and loose pajama-type pants with a colorful floral print. I introduced her to Mike. She later asked me, "So who's Mike?" I told her Mike was my partner. "Partners in what?" she asked. I explained that we were life partners; we lived together, shared our lives together. She reacted with surprise and, in future conversations, expressed disappointment. "Boy oh boy," she said more than once, "It's too bad Mike found you first, because if he hadn't, I would've never let you get by me." Seldom having had a relationship with a man that wasn't sexual, she was always worried that Mike would be jealous of the time I spent with her and wanted me to be clear that she would never come between us.

We went into church—Lillian, Mike, and I—and found a seat where I usually like to sit near the front. Lillian wasn't as awed by the sacred space as I would have hoped and commented rather loudly on anything around us that captured her interest. But she soon settled into the liturgy, remaining silent during hymns and congregational responses. She remained seated in the pew as we went forward for communion. At the end of the service, she leaned over to me and whispered that she was intrigued by our church. She noticed others going forward up into the chancel at the post-lude to watch the organist play. I asked if she wanted to do the same, and she responded enthusiastically to the suggestion. We hurried forward where she grabbed an empty seat in the chancel and watched the organist with rapt attention. After the dramatic finale, she applauded wildly, shouting, "Bravo, bravo" and "Encore!"

At the next Wednesday lunch, Lillian asked if Mike and I could pick her up before church, since the bus didn't run as often on Sundays, and I said we would. She began coming to church with us almost every Sunday. It was always something of a challenge for me. We used to arrive fifteen minutes early so she could have a cup of coffee, but I soon learned that she had barely taken one or two sips of coffee before it became time to go into church, and she would not be hurried. Once we didn't enter the sanctuary until halfway into the first hymn and found that our usual seats near the front had been taken. We had to find seats halfway back. She complained through the whole service about that because she couldn't see or hear as well. Thereafter, we picked her up earlier and I tried to impress upon her that if we wanted our seats near the front, we'd have to find our places ten minutes before the service began.

One Sunday we found seats in the fifth or sixth row during the organ prelude. Lillian was chatty that morning and began to comment (somewhat loudly) about others she saw around her. The well-dressed couple sitting in front of us looked at each other and, without a word, got up and moved to another pew. On another Sunday, I went into church alone while Lillian finished her coffee, telling her I'd save her a place in our usual spot. I sat in the middle of the pew and another gentleman was seated at the end of the pew by the aisle. Lillian hurried in as the prelude was ending and pushed her way past the man on the aisle. He commented that he was saving the place next to him for his wife. Lillian gave him a withering look and said, "How fat do you think I am? I'm not going to take up that much room." She took a few more steps. "Fuck'm," she uttered audibly as she took her seat next to me.

As the service began, I rehearsed over and over in my head the lecture I would give Lillian about appropriate behavior and language in church. I never delivered that lecture, but my face must have registered my exasperation. Later that week, over coffee, Lillian talked about how she thought about being a better person and how she was trying not to say the f-word as often as she was accustomed to doing. I softened in my feelings toward her.

Picking Lillian up for church became a fairly regular thing for several weeks. One Sunday, when we were away, she made it to church by herself and sat on the other side of the nave with her friends, the Wednesday coffee servers Jack and Jerry. She really liked that Sunday, because Jack and Jerry sat very close to the front, and Lillian could see everything up close.

One day the following week, Lillian invited me to her apartment. She lived in Gladstone Plaza, a six-story subsidized apartment building for low-income people about eight or nine blocks from the church. I told her when I would arrive, and she was waiting for me on the sidewalk, in front of the entrance, enjoying a cigarette. Since it was a secure building, she had to let me in with her key fob. After finishing her cigarette, she put her index finger to her lips, and giving a dismissive glance toward a few other tenants hanging out at the front of the building, told me not to talk to them, because they were "nosies" and it was nobody's business who came to see her. Taking the elevator to the sixth floor, she made it clear that her neighbors were nosy "wing-nuts," prostitutes, and druggies.

In the sixth floor hall, she paused in front of her apartment for dramatic effect, then slowly opened the door to an incredible scene. The small apartment was somewhat dark (she didn't like to turn on lights to save on the electric bill) and every inch of space was covered with knick-knacks, posters, and movie memorabilia. Even her stove and kitchen countertops were covered with kitschy figurines. Her bathtub was full of VHS tapes, adding to the collections she had on shelves in her main room and bedroom.

Marilyn Monroe and Elvis figured prominently in the photos and posters hanging on the wall. On a later visit I counted at least one hundred images of Marilyn in poster, magazine clippings, or ceramic form around the apartment. I came to the realization that she was a hoarder. She had at least thirty pairs of shoes, although I had ever only seen her wear one pair. I once asked for scissors to open a box for her and discovered that she had at least thirty pairs of scissors but, again, she only ever used one pair. I once bought her two half-gallon cartons of orange juice, only to find that she had three unopened cartons in her refrigerator. However, she was not the usual hoarder. Everything had a special place in her apartment and everything was in its place.

A renovation project in her building was especially upsetting to her because there was often dust in the hallway. She nagged the construction crew into giving her a special dust mat for her front door with a sticky surface that lifted off the dust and grit on one's soles. Nevertheless, when entering the apartment, she took off her shoes and washed off the soles with a sponge in her kitchen sink.

Renovation, however, brought a construction crew. Ever the flirt, she struck up conversations with members of the crew when she went outside to smoke. One woman on the crew took a liking to her, and Lillian was especially enamored with the crew chief, a handsome, brawny, younger man who was nice to her. He would bring her a coffee every morning, and the crew set aside a special chair for Lillian when she came outside to visit and smoke while they were working.

She spoke often about better times in her life, living in Miami, going to Italy when she was young, her four marriages. The only marriage she regretted ending was to her second husband who gave her everything she asked for and treated her very well. But she wanted to go out and have a good time, and he just wanted to stay at home.

Taking her to the supermarket was always an experience. She had made a point of knowing just about everyone who worked there and had to stop and greet them. "Hey, Andy," she'd yell in her gravelly voice from twenty or thirty feet away, "what do you have that looks good today?"

"Hi, Lillian. Everything looks good. Come take a look."

She usually had a favorite checker, and she would let the checker know to keep her station open until she could go through her line. Connie, behind the deli counter, would have to come out and give her a hug. Mel in the produce section would give her a few free oranges. Carlos at the other end of the deli counter always knew that Lillian liked the dark meat on chicken and not chicken breasts. Jennifer behind the Starbucks counter knew that Lillian like her coffee in a double paper cup with three Sweet'n Lows.

I came to realize that paranoia was a significant part of Lillian's dysfunctional relationship with others in her building. She was convinced everyone in her building wanted to know her business and was saying bad things about her. Her insults and rude behavior to them pretty much made her fears a self-fulfilling prophecy.

She would occasionally make a friend with another resident, but eventually the friend would let her down and then she wanted nothing to do with them. She befriended Paula, a paraplegic on the floor below hers who had two caregivers that would come and go from her apartment. Paula had a wide-screen TV and would invite Lillian to watch movies and TV specials with her in her apartment. As with anyone who was nice to her, Lillian would become bolder in asking favors. One of Paula's caregivers once offered to throw Lillian's few items of laundry in with Paula's when she did hers, and Lillian began to count on that, being too frugal to spend the number of coins it took to operate the building washer and dryer. The building manager told Paula that Lillian was taking advantage of her friendship, and she tearfully told Lillian to stop coming to her apartment.

Truth is, she also took advantage of my friendship, asking me to take her to the grocery store and to coffee. Mike and I, as a combination birthday and Christmas present, took her twice to Tad's Chicken and Dumplings, a homey roadside restaurant about forty-five-minute drive from Portland. And because of her conversational skills—both bawdy and childlike at the same time—we always had a good time.

Eventually Mike and I, too, became tired of Lillian's demands, her uncharitable assessment of others, and bitter outlook on life. Overseas travel, time spent supporting members of our own family with emotional crises and health needs, and involvement in volunteer activities halted our interactions with Lillian for a time.

As I was starting to feel a little guilty for not having spoken to Lillian for a period of over a year, she called me, out of the blue. "Ha-allo? Is this Stephen?"

"Lillian! Hi. I've been thinking about you. It's good to hear your voice. How are you?"

"Lousy. When I was coming out of Safeway where the entrance slants up a little, I slipped on the wet pavement and fell on my ass. And I think I dislocated my shoulder, and I'm in a lot of pain."

"I'm so sorry to hear that. When did this happen?"

"It happened about two weeks ago. I thought about suing them, but my lawyer died five years ago."

The reason Lillian had to take a bus about a mile and a half to Safeway to buy her groceries was that her neighborhood supermarket had banned her because of shoplifting. She also bought her money orders there. Lillian didn't pay her bills with checks because she didn't have a checking account. Her account at US Bank was only for the purpose of holding money she set aside for her burial and having a place for her direct-deposit social security checks to go. At the first of the month, she withdrew her social security payment in cash, asking that they be put in three envelopes, twenty-dollar bills in one, ten-dollar bills in another, and fives and ones in the final envelope. Then she went directly to Walgreens to buy two cartons of Maverick cigarettes and to Safeway to buy money orders to pay her rent and electrical bill.

"So I was hoping," Lillian continued, "that maybe you could take me to Denny's for a coffee. I like their coffee." On these calls, she always had lots of other things to tell me, primarily gossip about the "wingnuts, druggies, and prostitutes" who were her neighbors. She complained about the people who were always takers but would never do anything for anyone else, ironically overlooking the fact that some of her neighbors could say that about her.

We made a date for coffee. I always made a point of calling her on my cell phone when I was about five minutes away from her building to give her time to get down to the front door. I couldn't buzz her apartment from the security door. All the other residents in the building were listed on the directory screen, but jealously relishing her privacy, Lillian didn't want her name listed. Instead, she met me outside each time, sitting twenty feet from the entrance to have a cigarette while she waited for me to arrive.

When I arrived, I was shocked at how thin she had become.

"Where the flock did you park?" she barked at me.

"Just there," I answered, pointing to my car, "just behind the red truck."

"Jezus-god. Why didn't you park here? I've been saving this spot for you."

"I can't park here, Lillian. It's right in front of a fire hydrant. I don't want to get a ticket."

"You won't get a ticket. Do you mean I have to walk all the way up there to get into the car?"

"No, when we're ready to go, I'll go bring the car up here." We had this argument every time I came.

I always paid for at least fifteen minutes of parking, because Lillian was never in a hurry. I knew she would have to finish her cigarette and complain at length about people in her building and the building management. "Ka-ching, ka-ching. They always only want one thing—your money. They're not at all interested in helping you. They won't do one thing for you. They only want your money. You better believe it."

I walked her to the curb and made sure she was hanging on to something while I went to get the car. At Denny's, we found a booth by the window and a pleasant but matter-of-fact waitress took our order. Lillian, as she always did, ordered her coffee black with three Sweet'n Lows. Lillian had a definite sweet tooth, and I learned that, on occasion, she would go a whole week living on coffee and Butterfinger candy bars. I was amazed she wasn't diabetic. She had stacks of Butterfingers, the super-large size, in her refrigerator and closet.

"Have you had lunch, Lillian?" I asked. "Would you also like something to eat?"

Invariably, Lillian would order pancakes—with extra syrup. Servers were always amused at Lillian and took a liking to her because of her brash but affectionate behavior toward them. "Hey, boobie," she might say, "could you please bring me some extra napkins? Please, honey?" Or it was extra Sweet'n Lows or extra butter or another fork or you name it, and invariably the server would smile and bring it. "Thank you, honey," would be her reply.

As it became harder for her to dress and go out, she would call me and ask me to pick up a few things for her at the grocery store. Invariably, there was always something wrong with my delivery. The Butterfingers were the small size, not the large. The plastic carton of watermelon pieces looked good on top but the pieces underneath weren't ripe. The topical pain cream was the wrong kind.

On one trip to Trader Joe's, it became immediately clear that I would soon not be able to take her anywhere. She managed to get around by holding tight to her wobbly little shopping stroller and grabbing my arm when she needed to reach toward a shelf. More than once she stopped and doubled over, wincing in pain. She once told me she had stomach cancer, although I wasn't sure whether that was the doctor's diagnosis or her own. I didn't think we would make it to the car in the parking lot and we stopped and waited for Mike to bring the car to us.

Returning her to her apartment, she immediately collapsed in her chair, while I unloaded groceries and put them away. I added the two bottles of tomato juice to two unopened bottles she still had in the refrigerator from another grocery run. (I found four more in her closet.) She summoned the strength to come and check my work, and moved things two inches to the left or three inches to the right if I hadn't put them in exactly the right place. She wanted a glass of tomato juice but didn't have the strength to lift the bottle out of the refrigerator. I poured a glass for her. I left alarmed and worried about her ability to survive by herself, not only by what I had just witnessed but also by her accounts of falls she had taken recently, including trips to the toilet when she didn't quite make it in time. I told Lillian I would find her some help. Lillian didn't protest, I think having come to the realization that she couldn't survive on her own.

I called a friend, a retired social worker, to ask where I should go to get help for Lillian. She called a contact she still had with the city housing bureau and called back to give me the names and numbers of two social service employees, one with the housing bureau and one with Adult Protective Services. I called both and shared my concerns. The helpful man with Adult Protective Services happened to know Lillian, having been a resident services coordinator in the building where she lived several years before. As I described her mobility problems, her falls, and her almost constant pain, he said, "It sounds like she needs to go to the hospital."

I knew Lillian hated the hospital, primarily because in previous visits they wouldn't let her smoke, but she also was slowly accepting the fact that she needed help. I talked with her about it, convincing her that she really needed to have a doctor check things out and perhaps give her something for her pain. She said yes, she wanted to go to the hospital. I immediately called the guy at Adult Protective Services, and the next day an ambulance came and took her to the local hospital.

I visited her almost every day, fetching things from her apartment which was only a few blocks away, bringing her a few Butterfingers (which she ate all in one day). She gave me her apartment key so I could let myself in and hide her cigarettes, ashtray, lighter, and air freshener in case of an inspection. She was not supposed to smoke in her apartment, but there wasn't a day that went by but what she opened her window wide and smoked while watching old movies on her VHS player.

Every day in her hospital bed, she complained about being there. "They treat me like a dog. They don't do a damn thing for me here. There's only one thing they want and that's your money." She wouldn't eat the food, not liking the way it was prepared and saying it was cold. She begged me to take her home.

"What would you do if I took you back to your apartment?" I asked.

"Sit in my chair."

"How would you get to the bathroom? How would you fix yourself something to eat? You can barely stand. I can't take you home until the doctor releases you."

She asked me to bring her just one cigarette.

"Lillian, they won't let you smoke here."

"They won't know."

Only one other person came to visit her, a woman who befriended her when coming to visit a girlfriend in her building. Lillian had no family left, and she had antagonized almost all of the people she lived with. She was angry with me and Linda, her other friend, because we wouldn't take her home. "If you were really my friend, you'd get me out of here." She suggested more than once that she could come live with Mike and me.

At each visit I was shocked to see how much more noticeably feeble Lillian had become. Linda found out from the doctor what CAT scans had revealed—cancer was present all through her body: lungs, stomach, liver, bones, and it was doubtful that she would make it through the week.

During my last visit, when she lay dying in her hospital bed, I sat by her bed, holding her hand and she whispered, "I love you." She had stopped worrying about her apartment and her Oregon ID card, and her bills, and the things in her refrigerator. She told me tearfully she didn't want to die, and I could see that she knew she was dying.

The hospital finally discharged her to a nursing home with hospice care. Mike and I drove to the nursing home the day after her transfer. Because of the COVID pandemic, we could not go in, but the kind receptionist took us around the outside of the building to her window. The nursing assistant in her room opened the window so we could wave and shout our greetings and good wishes at Lillian. She looked at us, but was otherwise unresponsive, under heavy pain medication and too weak to talk. She died the next morning.

So how should I think about my relationship to Lillian? What conclusions can I draw? She is not someone I would have chosen as a friend, but she is someone who became my friend and became prominent in my life for a time. I am reminded of something Malcolm Muggeridge once wrote: that we most often choose our friends not for what they mean to us but rather what we mean to them.

I am also reminded of a homily I heard given by Fr. John Scannell in which he stated that we often believe that good thinking leads to good acting, but—he reminded his listeners—it's just as often the case that good acting leads to good thinking. And this was my lesson in love. That love is an action verb, not a warm, fuzzy feeling. At times I was as much repulsed by Lillian as attracted to her, but I felt compelled to follow my baptismal covenant—to seek and serve Christ in all persons—and, in looking for the sacred in Lillian, found something I could love. I grew to love her, in the same way one can love a difficult child.

At her graveside, there were only four of us, Mike and I, and Linda and her girlfriend Kathy. Linda asked me if I wanted to say a prayer. I didn't have anything prepared, but simply put my hand on her casket and said, "Lord, into your hands we commend your child, Lillian." We left knowing that Lillian was now free of pain, free of fear, and we hoped she would find something holy and life-giving that she could embrace on the other side.

Chapter 6

Q. What is redemption?

A. Redemption is the act of God which sets us free from the power of evil, sin, and death.

Q. What is the great importance of Jesus's suffering and death?

A. By his obedience, even to suffering and death, Jesus made the offering which we could not make; in him we are freed from the power of sin and reconciled to God.

Untangling Atonement

THE PRIEST GAVE A quick shudder after saying the words "propitiatory atonement," suggesting that was a harmful theological teaching that one should not give much credence to. I happened to be sitting in a catechesis class when she made the dismissive remark, and she quickly moved on to another topic.

I was perplexed. In my evangelical upbringing, Christ's atonement for our sins had been a foundational teaching. It never occurred to me that a Christian, let alone a priest, should take exception to it. Can one simply dismiss a religious teaching just because one finds it distasteful?

Propitiate means to appease or pacify. The argument goes like this: we, all of us, have sinned, and righteousness and justice demand that the price of that sin has to be paid. The apostle Paul tells us in Rom 6 that "the wages of sin is death." According to theologians like J. Clement Connell, sin is personal rebellion against God, which rightly incurs God's punishment. Christ, however, made substitutionary atonement, paying the price of sin in his death on the cross to appease a righteous God's wrath.[2]

The principal disagreement seems to be with the belief in an anthropomorphic portrayal of an angry, vengeful God who condemns those who transgress to death, rather than a God who loves all creation and is ready to forgive. Certainly, references in the Hebrew Scriptures create such an image. For example, "The Lord said to Moses, 'I have seen this people, how stiff-necked they are. Now let me alone, so that my wrath may burn hot against them and I may consume them'" (Exod 32:9–10). The Bible tells us that God was angry with Moses (Deut 4:21), Solomon (1 Kgs 11:9), King Amaziah (2 Chr 25:15), and many times with the people of Israel (e.g., Exod 32:11), among others.

A second objection is to the notion of a blood sacrifice, a very pagan rite, not part of an enlightened way of dealing with moral failures or spiritual obligations. According to the religious historian, Karen Armstrong, animal sacrifice was a universal religious practice in the ancient world.[3] Ancient peoples held a strong conviction that life and death, creativity and destruction were inextricably entwined. There could be no life without a sacrificial death.

Richard Rohr described substitutionary atonement as a Christian belief that has done a great deal of damage.[4] He claims that this violent theory of redemption has given legitimacy to punitive and violent solutions all the way down—from papacy to parenting. I learned, while reading Rohr, that—according to at least

2. Connell, "Propitiatory Element," 28–42.

3. Armstrong, *Great Transformation*, xv.

4. Rohr, *Things Hidden*, 202.

one scholar—the substitutionary understanding of Jesus's death was not central in the first thousand years of Christianity and its first articulation only happened just over nine hundred years ago in 1098 in St. Anselm's treatise *Cur Deus Homo*.[5] I was puzzled by this claim since Scripture and our liturgy is full of references to Christ's sacrifice for our sins.

Scripture has many references to sacrifice as atonement for sin, both in the Hebrew Scriptures (e.g., Lev 5:6: "And you shall bring to the Lord, as your penalty for the sin that you have committed, a female from the flock, a sheep or a goat, as a sin-offering; and the priest shall make atonement on your behalf for your sin") and in the New Testament, with specific reference to Christ (Rom 3:24: "They are now justified by his grace as a gift, through the redemption that is in Christ Jesus, whom God put forward as a sacrifice of atonement by his blood, effective through faith"). In the book of Leviticus alone, over forty references are made to sacrifice as atonement for sin.

Liturgy, too, is full of references to Christ's atonement for our sins. Familiar examples include

- "Lamb of God, you take away the sin of the world."

- "He stretched out his arms upon the cross, and offered himself, in obedience to your will, a perfect sacrifice for the whole world."

- "We celebrate the memorial of our redemption, O Father . . ."

- "Christ our Passover is sacrificed for us."

The Eucharist is itself a celebration of Christ's sacrifice for us.

One of my clergy friends (admitting that it is a radical theory) holds that Jesus was killed because he spoke truth to power, and it was only later that all the theories about atonement were created. However, her belief overlooks the number of references to redemption and Christ's sacrificial atonement in Scripture and the evidence that atonement was the teaching of the early church.

5. Borg, "Christianity Divided."

Even in earliest church history was the view that something objectively substantial in Christ's death is necessarily connected with forgiveness and acceptance before God.[6] Textual evidence for this has ranged from AD 130 to the late second century. The anonymous writer of *Epistle to Diognetus* wrote,

> He did not hate us or reject us, or bear a grudge against us; instead, he was patient and forbearing; in his mercy he took upon himself our sin; he himself gave us his own Son as a ransom for us, the holy one for the lawless, the guiltless for the guilty, "the just for the unjust," the incorruptible for the corruptible, the immortal for the mortal. For what else but his righteousness could have covered our sins?[7]

And Justin Martyr (ca. 100–165) saw clearly in Scripture that there was no salvation without the death of Christ and faith in him.

Peter Abelard (1079–1142) shifted discussions of the atonement from requirements of the justice and wrath of God to its affecting influence on the human spirit, initiating the *moral influence* view of atonement. According to Abelard, the manner in which God demonstrated his justice in the death of Christ was "to show forth his love to us, or to convince us how much we ought to love him who 'spared not his own Son' for us."[8]

Cynthia Bourgeault also makes the argument that God wasn't angry. Yes, Jesus died for our sins, but he died on behalf of a collective fallen human condition. It was the ultimate act of kenosis in which he "implanted himself deeply at ground zero."[9] He died to insulate us from death's sting and empower us to live within our flesh as he himself had lived, being resurrected to new life in him.

I think there is another possibility that addresses our individual as well as collective sin. Jesus died not because an angry God demanded it, but because humans, somewhere in our collective unconscious, demand atonement. In contradiction to the

6. Nettles, "History and Theories."

7. As cited in Nettles, "History and Theories."

8. Abelard, "Epistle to the Romans," 279, 283.

9. Bourgeault, *Wisdom Jesus*, 107.

Leviticus Scriptures, other Scriptures suggest that God does not—never did—demand sacrifice. The psalmist writes,

> I bring no charges against you concerning your sacrifices
>   or concerning your burnt offerings, which are ever before me.
> I have no need of a bull from your stall
>   or of goats from your pens,
> for every animal of the forest is mine,
>   and the cattle on a thousand hills . . .
> . . . Do I eat the flesh of bulls
>   or drink the blood of goats? (Ps 50:8–10, 13)

From Hosea, these words: "For I desire steadfast love and not sacrifice, the knowledge of God rather than burnt offerings" (Hos 6:6). The writer of Hebrews states: "It is impossible for the blood of bulls and goats to take away sins . . . .Day after day every priest stands and performs his religious duties; again and again he offers the same sacrifices, which can never take away sins" (Heb 10:4,11).

And yet, atonement remains in our collective unconscious. Armstrong writes that human sacrifice was common in the ancient world, even among the pre-Israel Canaanites. The firstborn child was often regarded as the offspring, and therefore property, of a god and had to be returned to that deity in sacrifice to ensure the circulation of power in the cosmos.[10]

Thus, the story of Abraham and Isaac. As the story in Genesis goes, God gave the shocking command for Abraham to take his only son Isaac to a mountain in the land of Moriah and there offer him as a burnt sacrifice. After Abraham had built the altar, bound his son, and laid him on the altar, and just as he raised the knife, an angel appeared to him, telling him to spare his son and sacrifice a nearby ram instead. God provided another sacrifice.

That same archetype from society's collective unconscious is evident today in a predominantly punitive, rather than restorative, justice system. We demand atonement for wrongs. Amnesty International recorded at least 1,477 death sentences in fifty-four countries in 2020.[11] Every day, people are executed and sentenced

10. Armstrong, *Great Transformation,* 94.
11. Amnesty International, "Death Penalty."

to death by the state as punishment for a variety of crimes—sometimes for acts that should not be criminalized. Perhaps, then, Christ offered himself as a sacrifice for the whole world not to appease God's wrath over our sins, but to appease the human demand for atonement. In his sacrifice, he gave of himself in a way that said, "Okay, this is it. It is finished. I am giving my life for the sins of the world. No more sacrifice—animal or human—is required." And he went even further. He demonstrated by his resurrection that new life can arise from a fallen state.

Christ's death puts the seal on the fact that Jesus was fully human, experiencing all that humans experience, even to the extreme of suffering, torture, and death, what Cynthia Bourgeault calls "the sacramental necessity that Jesus drink to the dregs the full anguish of the human condition."[12] And being sinless, having committed no offense large or small, he was the perfect sacrificial offering to dispel the notion of sacrifice to appease an angry God. Here is a representation of God unlike any other god, who gave up his sovereignty not only to establish unity with humanity, but also to share with us his unity with God. In his death, he put to death any notion that we have a debt to settle with our maker.

In response, we are inclined to give God something in return, but not a sacrifice of atonement. We desire to offer our sacrifice of thanksgiving, both in the remembrance of Christ's death and celebration of his real presence that we do when his followers gather together (*eucharist* means "thanksgiving"), and in the grateful sacrifice of our lives. We look for ways to grow into the kind of self-giving example he set. We look for his image in the people we interact with each day. We seek unity with a loving God and the long view of a life that is eternal.

12. Bourgeault, *Wisdom Jesus*, 118.

Chapter 7

Q. What are the creeds?

A. The creeds are statements of our basic beliefs about God.

We Believe

I HAVE ALWAYS BELIEVED in God, although that confidence was fragile at times. As a young child I had an unusual transcendent experience in which I felt very keenly God's presence and I've never had serious reason to doubt God's existence since then. (That's not to say I haven't had occasion to question other stuff the church has taught.) Some, like me, have had a "born again" experience; others gradually grow into a life of faith through acculturation in a faith community, their own experiences with God, and participation in the sacraments.

As a relatively new Episcopalian, I was somewhat nonplussed when a good friend admitted that she sometimes was inclined to cross her fingers when she said the Nicene Creed during the Eucharist on Sunday mornings. At first, it was disconcerting to me how many Episcopalians I'd come to know who had all sorts of beliefs concerning the nature of God, the virgin birth, the resurrection, and other things I thought were nonnegotiables when it came to Christian faith. Now it gives me great joy every Sunday to witness these same people, all of us in a different place on our spiritual path, say the Creed together and gather around the Lord's table as part of my spiritual family, the body of Christ.

An honest appraisal of one's beliefs makes room for doubt. Doubt is not unbelief; it is uncertain belief. In 1916 James Snowden defined it as "the borderland between knowledge and ignorance, the twilight between light and darkness."[1] He went on to say that not only is doubt not a hindrance to our thinking, but it is a highly useful factor in our knowledge and in life. "Doubt is the great destroyer of error, the scythe that mows down the weeds of baleful beliefs, the scavenger that removes the corpses of false hopes and dead faiths."[2] Scriptures are filled with examples of men and women challenging, questioning, and demanding answers from God. I didn't come to a more mature, deeply held faith until I began to question and wrestle with teaching that didn't make sense to me. Like the distraught father who brought his epileptic son to Jesus, I could say in my darkest times, "I believe; help my unbelief!" (Mark 9:24).

Tish Harrison Warren writes that sometimes trusting God feels to her like a steep climb. She writes,

> In times of deep pain in my own life, the belief of the church has carried me. When we confess the creeds in worship, we don't say, "I believe in God the Father . . ." because some weeks I do and some weeks, I can't climb that high. Instead we confess, "We believe . . ." Belief isn't a feeling inside of us, but a reality outside of us into which we enter, and when we find our faith faltering, sometimes all we can do is fall on the faith of the saints. We believe together.[3]

The Nicene Creed was written about three centuries after Jesus's ministry on earth. It was the product of months of heated debate and negotiation. In spite of the fact that minority opinions

1. Snowden, "Place of Doubt," 151–55.
2. Snowden, "Place of Doubt," 151–52.
3. Warren, *Prayer in the Night*, 87.

were sometimes violently suppressed and arguments led to some fifty years of acrimony, the members of the Council of Nicaea did codify a set of beliefs that was by then the majority opinion among the Christian community, largely thanks to the widespread popularity of Paul's letters to the Church in diaspora.[4] As Diana Butler Bass points out, the creed developed in the context of a community's living, transformative, prayer-filled, and active spiritual life—not the other way around,[5] meaning the creed is really the product and *symbol* of faith, not the faith itself.

The religious historian Karen Armstrong maintains that, in the early church, faith was a matter of practical insight and active commitment. It had little to do with abstract belief, dogma, or theology.[6] The word translated as "faith" in the Christian texts is the Greek *pistis* (and its verbal form *pisteuo*), which means "trust; loyalty; engagement; commitment."[7] When translating the Greek into Latin, Saint Jerome used the Latin verb *credo*, meaning "I give my heart." Over time the English word *believe* has changed its meaning from the original Middle English *bileven*, meaning "to prize, value, hold dear."

So then, if—as Armstrong maintains—faith has historically been more a matter of practice than belief, is the Creed important? The answer has to be yes; belief is not irrelevant to our practice. We meet every Sunday, participate in the sacraments, and try as best we can to love our neighbor as ourselves because we believe in (i.e., trust, commit, give our heart to) Jesus, his teaching and example. Creed comes from that word *credo*. As the community of believers, we recite to God and to each other, the foundational principles upon which we ground our faith practice. We do so acknowledging that our comprehension of these mysteries is imperfect.

The Creed certainly does not cover all our personally held religious beliefs. A Christian health worker in Oregon asked for a religious exemption from a COVID vaccine mandate, citing

4. Aslan, *Zealot*, 213–214.

5. Bass, *Christianity after Religion*, 131.

6. Armstrong, *Case for God*, 102.

7. Armstrong, *Case for God*, 87.

Scripture on his request form. "I have a very strong conviction that if I feel like I should not put something in my body, I shouldn't do it," said the health worker. "In Romans it talks about not eating anything that goes against your conscience and that would be similar to injecting something into your body," he said.[8] He was denied his religious exemption. He didn't understand that personal discomfort was not the same as an article of faith.

According to a study conducted by Lifeway Research in 2019, six in ten Americans affirm that religious belief is about *personal opinion* rather than *objective truth*,[9] which led the author of the article to wonder whether we create God in our own image. This finding points to the value of defining what we as a faith community believe. The early translators of Scripture used the word *credo*, not the Latin word *opinor*, from which we derive the word "opinion." Our corporate beliefs—those to which we give our heart to as the body of Christ—do not include the many personal opinions represented among its members—about who God is, or politics, or vaccinations, or anything else.

I have continuing questions, primarily in terms of things I don't understand, because ours is a faith of paradoxes and mysteries, things we may never fully understand. The virgin birth seems to contradict the laws of human biology. I don't understand how a resurrection could take place, but I understand the significance of a risen Christ in my own life. So, with conviction, I stand with members of my church family on Sunday morning after the sermon and boldly proclaim those truths in the Creed, not as personal opinions, but as a faith I've entered into and come to trust.

8. Severance, "Unvaccinated Legacy Workers."
9. Kellum, "Importance of Creeds."

Chapter 8

Q. Who is the Holy Spirit?

A. The Holy Spirit is the Third Person of the Trinity, God at work in the world and in the Church even now.

The Holy Spirit

YOU MAY HAVE EXPERIENCED the Holy Spirit. You may be singing a familiar hymn in church, and suddenly you are moved by the words that suddenly have a deeper meaning than you realized previously. Perhaps you are sitting in a committee meeting with fellow parishioners and you all sense a spirit of consensus and assurance that the decision you have reached together is in keeping with God's will. You are listening to a sermon or a guest speaker at a Sunday forum, and you have the feeling that the speaker's words were intended for you and were exactly the thing you needed to hear. You are sitting by a river in a beautiful valley and are overwhelmed by the beauty of the place and the sense of God's presence. You wake up thinking about someone in need and feel compelled to call or visit that person.

Richard Rohr describes the Holy Spirit as that aspect of God that works secretly, largely from within at the deepest levels of our desiring. It is an inner compass, a "homing device" in our soul, "an implanted desire that calls us to our foundation and our future."[1] Metaphors of the Holy Spirit in Scripture include wind, fire, a descending dove, and flowing water. Michael Horton emphasizes that the Holy Spirit is not our spirit, and its voice is not to be confused with our own. Rather, the Holy Spirit is the presence who works *within* us, even to the point of indwelling us and interceding in our hearts.[2]

Hauerwas and Willimon maintain that the Holy Spirit has been given short shrift in the theology of the Christian West.[3] Not much is said in either the Apostles' and Nicene Creeds about the third person of the Trinity, and it lacks any kind of prominence in contemporary theology. The Nicene Creed simply states that the Holy Spirit is the giver of life who proceeds from the Father and the Son, is worshiped and glorified, and has spoken through the prophets. The Apostles' Creed says much less, mentioning the Holy Spirit only in passing.

Hebrew Scriptures tell us the Holy Spirit existed as part of God from the beginning, mentioned in Genesis in the very second verse of the Bible. While the earth was a formless void and darkness covered the face of the deep, a wind from God—also translated as the spirit of God—swept over the face of the waters.

And centuries before Christ, God spoke to the prophet Joel, declaring the day of the Lord was coming and proclaiming, "I will pour out my spirit on all flesh; your sons and your daughters shall prophesy, your old men shall dream dreams, and your young men shall see visions" (Joel 2:28). The Gospel of Matthew and our Creed tell us that Jesus was conceived in the Virgin Mary by the Holy Spirit.

In John's Gospel, Jesus comforts his disciples before his arrest and crucifixion by saying that God the Father would send an advocate in Christ's name, the Holy Spirit, who "will teach you everything, and remind you of all that I have said to you" (John 14:26).

1. Rohr, *Falling Upward*, 88–90.

2. Horton, *Rediscovering the Holy Spirit*, 26.

3. Hauerwas and Willimon, *Holy Spirit*, 5–6.

After Jesus's resurrection and ascension, the Holy Spirit's dramatic debut, if you will, happened among followers of the Way, gathered together in the room of a house. The writer of Acts (most say it was Luke) says that there was suddenly from heaven a sound like the rush of a violent wind that filled the entire house where they were sitting. Something appearing as tongues of fire hovered above each of them and they began to speak in other languages, as the Spirit gave them ability (Acts 2:1–4). Having heard the sound, a crowd of Jews from other countries gathered in front of the house and was bewildered, because each one heard the disciples preaching in the native language of each listener.

The Holy Spirit was dramatically at work in the early church. Luke and Paul make frequent reference to this member of the Trinity in their epistles. On the day of Pentecost, after the speaking in tongues and an inspiring sermon by Peter, many in the gathered crowd welcomed his message and were baptized. According to Acts, about three thousand persons were added to the followers of the Way that day. "They devoted themselves to the apostles' teaching and fellowship, to the breaking of bread and the prayers" (Acts 2:42). Acts makes frequent reference to the Holy Spirit in the courage of the disciples to preach and heal and bear witness of the gospel to skeptical leaders. Paul wrote to the church in Rome that it is the Holy Spirit that pours God's love into our hearts (Rom 5:5), intercedes for us when we don't know how to pray (Rom 8:26), and leads us from fear into confidence as children of God (Rom 8:14–16).

The earliest Christians spoke of the Holy Spirit as a feminine figure. Many early Christian authors—in particular, those who had been practicing Jews—spoke of the Holy Spirit as Mother.[4] An essential reason for this practice is the fact that the Hebrew word for Spirit, *ruach*, is in nearly all cases feminine. Also in Aramaic, the word for Spirit, *rucha*, is feminine. The first Christians, all of whom were Jews, took on this practice.

The Holy Spirit is at work in the church today. As Hauerwas and Willimon put it:

4. Van Oort, "Holy Spirit as Feminine."

> Christians believe the countercultural, peculiar claim
> that *through the Spirit* God is active in history then and
> now. . . . The Spirit did not stop working after the first
> days of the church; the Spirit is present in all times and
> places, making Christ known, and in our baptism makes
> us participants in a story initiated and sustained by the
> Holy Spirit.[5]

The Greek Orthodox prelate and theologian John Zizioulas maintains that the Holy Spirit is "the person of the Trinity who actually
realizes in history that which we call Christ," our Savior.[6] Saint
Augustine wrote, "what the soul is to the body of man, that the
Holy Spirit is to the Body of Christ, which is the Church."[7]

From the late sixties to early seventies, my friends and I were
curious about and somewhat caught up in what was then called
"charismatic renewal" (*charisma* meaning a special spiritual gift
or power conferred by the Holy Spirit). Although Pentecostal-
ism grew in popularity earlier in the twentieth century, the new
charismatic surge began in an Episcopal church, where, on April 3,
1960, Rector Dennis Bennett stood and shared how the Holy Spirit
was at work in his life.[8] The movement then experienced dramatic
growth throughout the world within mainstream bodies such as
Roman Catholics, Episcopalians, and other Protestant denomina-
tions. Advocates of the movement promoted the experience of the
Holy Spirit as manifested in spiritual gifts (especially speaking in
tongues and healing).

With a friend, I attended emotionally charged services where
I witnessed those who spoke in tongues, or interpreted the message conveyed in tongues, or occasionally were "slain in the Spirit,"
apparently so overcome by the Holy Spirit during the laying on
of hands that they passed out, falling into the arms of those ready
to assist them. Then (as now) I tended to shy away from dramatic

5. Hauerwas and Willimon, *Holy Spirit*, 23.

6. Zizioulas, *Being as Communion*, 110–11.

7. Augustine, as quoted by Huston Smith, *Soul of Christianity*, 86.

8. Baker, "Charismatic Movement."

expressions of emotion but was somewhat curious and envious of those who could experience such ecstasy.

After one such service, alone in my apartment, I knelt by my bed and, as instructed, lifted my hands and asked for the infilling of the Holy Spirit. After a few moments of prayer, I opened my mouth and began to babble, amazed that I could put together strings of syllables that sounded much like a secret language. However, I didn't feel any ecstasy or even a new, keen awareness. I got up from my knees feeling not much different. The next day I decided that this may not be the charisma that God wanted to give me. What I overlooked at the time was the fact that, being a follower of Jesus, I already had the gift of the Spirit. In the years since then, I often have felt the presence of God in the beauty that surrounds me, in fellowship with other Christians, in inspiring music and liturgy, and in being called to serve others.

It is good to remember that God did not come to Elijah in a dramatic way. God did not appear in a strong wind, an earthquake, or a fire, but rather in "a sound of sheer silence" (1 Kgs 19:11–12). The signs I should have looked for and have come to appreciate since then are what the Apostle Paul referred to as the "fruit of the Spirit": love, joy, peace, patience, kindness, generosity, faith-fulness, gentleness, and self-control (Gal 5:22–23). Our ability to love the stranger and see the Christ in others is a gift of the Spirit. And, as we like sheep are prone to wander, it is the Holy Spirit that intercedes on our behalf and draws us ever so gently but insistently back into fellowship with God.

Chapter 9

Q. *How do we recognize the presence of the Holy Spirit in our lives?*

A. *We recognize the presence of the Holy Spirit when we confess Jesus Christ as Lord and are brought into love and harmony with God, with ourselves, with our neighbors, and with all creation.*

Real Life on a Bus

SEVERAL YEARS AGO, I was riding the bus home from the university, in a window seat just in front of the stairwell by the back exit doors. Riding the bus was routine for me, and I no longer was much interested in the familiar neighborhoods and landmarks I passed every day. To alleviate my boredom, it was my habit to carry in my satchel professional articles or a book that I could read on the way home.

However, that night, I did look up often enough to realize it was a lovely fall evening and the sky was touched with a little color from the setting sun hitting the shelf of clouds overhead. I was reading *Monk Habits for Everyday People* by Dennis Okholm,[1] the section of his first chapter where he talks about "real life." He was contrasting the quiet bliss of a retreat in the monastery with the return to the daily hurriedness and noise of the work world. Which was real? I was uncomfortable with the dichotomy, recalling Norvene Vest's point (interpreting Saint Benedict) that we can experience the sacred in the ordinary.[2]

Just as I was thinking these thoughts, a voice behind me, at the back of the bus, began singing. A young woman was just singing very softly to herself, but in an unself-conscious way. She had a lovely, pure voice and was singing in another language (something eastern European, I think). None of the passengers said a word; all just sat quietly and, like me I suspected, listened.

A quiet peacefulness pervaded the bus. I had to look up from my book, look out the window, and just surrender to the music and the evening's rosy light, relishing the beautiful moment. And I thought, this is a moment of grace; this is where God brings a moment of pure beauty into one of life's more mundane experiences (riding a bus).

After a few stops someone behind me got off and, not hearing the singing again, I realized it must have been the woman who sang. It was a shame because I wanted to thank her for singing. I was never more aware of the sacred within the ordinary. I rode the rest of the way home thanking God for the unexpected beauty in real life.

C. S. Lewis wrote, "The world is crowded with God. He walks everywhere incognito. And the incognito is not always hard to penetrate. The real labour is to remember, to attend. In fact, to come awake."[3]

1. Okholm, *Monk Habits*.

2. Vest, *Preferring Christ*, 102.

3. Lewis, *Letters to Malcolm*, 75.

Chapter 10

Q. *What are the Holy Scriptures?*

A. *The Holy Scriptures, commonly called the Bible, are the books of the Old and New Testaments.*

Q. *Why do we call the Holy Scriptures the Word of God?*

A. *We call them the Word of God because God inspired their human authors and because God still speaks to us through the Bible.*

Holy Scriptures

THE BIBLE IS A very wonderful and difficult book. To Christians it is the word of God. Its pages reveal the story of our faith and, in vivid language, unfold the eternal struggle between good and evil, the Creator's attempts to reach out to the human creation, and the supreme manifestation of divine love in the person of Jesus Christ. Biblical texts were written over a period of hundreds of years in which the living conditions and cultures of its writers varied considerably: nomadic existence, established kingdoms, periods of exile, fierce oppression, and cosmopolitan Hellenistic education.

The time span of its composition encompasses the age of Homer to the extension of the Roman empire into parts of Scotland (84 CE).[1]

The Bible has had a profound influence on literature and a culture of literacy, especially in the Western world, being the first book printed on a press with moveable type by Johannes Gutenberg in the 1450s. Other fun facts about the Bible include:

- Its total sales are estimated to be over five billion copies, making it the bestselling book of all time.

- It is also the most frequently shoplifted book.[2]

- It has been translated into nearly 700 languages.[3]

- It is the source of many of our common expressions, such as "salt of the earth," "forbidden fruit," and "cross to bear."

The first part of the Bible (or as Christians have traditionally referred to it, the Old Testament) is a collection of ancient religious writings comprised primarily of the books of the Hebrew Bible, written by various authors. The Bible's second part (Christian Testament, or New Testament) is a series of accounts and letters that discuss the life and teachings of Jesus, as well as events in the first-century early church.

Most scholars today agree that the stories and laws of the Hebrew Bible were communicated orally, through prose and poetry, over centuries. When they were transcribed, text was written in columns upon a strip of papyrus or parchment, twenty to thirty feet long, and wound onto a stick. This papyrus roll was called a *biblios*. Our Bible was originally *ta biblia* (the rolls).[4] According to Karen Armstrong, it was the prophet Ezra who, at the beginning of the fourth century BCE, gathered together the collection of stories, scrolls, and miscellaneous teachings by various authors into what became the Torah, the five books that comprise the first part of the

1. Riches, *Bible*, 9.
2. Zeitlin, "24 Surprising Facts."
3. Pruitt, "Who Wrote the Bible?," para. 2.
4. Durant, *Life of Greece*, 206.

Hebrew Bible.[5] Ezra created a spiritual discipline around these sacred texts, elevating it above all other writings at the time and calling it "the law of Moses." Over time other texts were added to the sacred collection: teachings of the prophets, historical narratives, poetry and wisdom writings. Beginning in the seventh century BCE, different groups of authors, at different times, wrote down these texts. They were not combined into the single work we know today as the Old Testament until probably the first century BCE.[6]

The first four books of the Christian Testament, the stories of Jesus's life, have become the central documents in the Christian faith. Scholars believe they were written beginning around AD 70, about forty years after Jesus was crucified.[7] Like the Hebrew Scriptures, these stories were most probably communicated orally over the years before they were collected and written down. We don't know that the books of the Christian Testament were always written by the people to whom they are attributed. The names that were attached to the titles of the Gospels (e.g., "the Gospel according to Matthew") were later additions provided by editors and scribes according to who they thought were the authors.

As a young man, after years of hearing Bible stories, participating in Bible studies, and following along as the Sunday readings were read in church, it occurred to me that I should read the entire Bible from beginning to end. I started with Gen 1. The ancient stories with their familiar characters carried me through that book and the next. And then I came to Leviticus and verses like this:

> If your offering is a goat, you shall bring it before the Lord and lay your hand on its head; it shall be slaughtered before the tent of meeting; and the sons of Aaron shall dash its blood against all sides of the altar. You shall present as your offering from it, as an offering by fire to the Lord, the fat that covers the entrails, and all the fat that is around the entrails; the two kidneys with the fat

5. Armstrong, *Bible*, 32–34.

6. Pruitt, "Who Wrote the Bible?," para. 9.

7. Pruitt, "Who Wrote the Bible?," para. 12.

that is on them at the loins, and the appendage of the liver.[8]

Page after page talked about burnt offerings, grain offerings, sin offerings, and blood sacrifices of different kinds, not to mention rules about clean and unclean animals, purification rites, bodily discharges, and sexual relations. I gave up.

But later in life I discovered there are a few wonderful parts to Leviticus. As tedious as much of it is, it also contains this instruction: "When an alien resides with you in your land, you shall not oppress the alien. The alien who resides with you shall be to you as the citizen among you; you shall love the alien as yourself, for you were aliens in Egypt" (Lev 19:33–34). The roots of twenty-first-century social justice are found in those ancient texts, as well as in Jesus's teachings.

The Bible portrays all aspects of life, good and bad. I was well into adulthood before I realized that not all psalms were comforting or uplifting. There are a number of complaining and cursing verses among them, for example "Surely you will strike all my enemies across the face, you will break the teeth of the wicked" (Ps 3:7). On the other hand, who doesn't take inspiration from "The Lord is my shepherd; I shall not be in want" or "The heavens declare the glory of God, and the firmament shows his handiwork"? Who hasn't been perplexed by some of Jesus's parables, but then inspired by the sermon on the mount? The writer Paul may say in 1 Corinthians that women should be silent in church and not permitted to speak (14:34), but then he writes in Galatians "There is no longer . . . male and female; for all of you are one in Christ Jesus" (3:28).

What is disconcerting to many are the seeming contradictions in the Bible. Of the two accounts of creation in the first two chapters of Genesis, which is the accurate order of things? How many women gathered at Jesus's tomb on the first day of the week: one, two, or three? For centuries, Jews and Christians read the Bible reverently as a largely allegorical text, grounded in a long

8. Lev 3:12–15 NRSV

oral tradition, its stories passed down by word of mouth from one generation to another.[9] Literal interpretation of Scripture is a historically recent development, a nineteenth-century phenomenon.

Esther DeWaal explores the issue of contradictions as well as the many paradoxes in Scripture.[10] She lists several of these conundrums: for example, a God who also becomes a man, a victor who rides on a donkey in his hour of triumph, a king who says his kingdom is not on earth, our strength is in our weakness, in losing my life I will find it.

How seriously should we consider the Bible? What place should it hold in contemporary faith? Diana Butler Bass reported that, compared to young Americans fifty years ago, today's young people believe the Bible to be less sacred, less accurate, equal to other sacred texts, and more influenced by mistakes of human opinion and transmission. And yet, as Benedict said in the sixth century, "For what page or what utterance of the divinely inspired books of the Old and New Testaments is not a most unerring rule for human life?"[11] In his book, *The Second Mountain*, David Brooks writes about his journey to faith. As a child in Hebrew school, he learned all the biblical stories—Noah and the ark, Jonah and the whale, David and Goliath—which performed the function of myth, helping him understand right and wrong. As a young man he studied them as wisdom literature, tools for understanding the problems of life. But over the decades, things began to change imperceptibly. He writes,

> I think what changed, in the most incremental, boring way possible, is that at some point I had the sensation that these stories are not fabricated tales happening to other, possibly fictional people: They are the underlying shape of reality. They are renditions of the recurring patterns of life. They are the scripts we repeat.[12]

9. Armstrong, *Bible*, 3.

10. DeWaal, *Living with Contradiction*, 24.

11. Doyle, *Benedict's Rule*, ch. 73.

12. Brooks, *Second Mountain*, 211–12.

In other words, the very conundrums, paradoxes, and contradictions that perplex us are the very things that engage us, drawing us deeper into the understanding the realities of life and the mysteries of our faith. Rowan Williams writes, "Bible reading is an essential part of the Christian life because Christian life is a listening life. The Christian listens for God and listens in the company of other believers to those texts that, from the very beginnings of the Christian community, have been identified as carrying the voice of God."[13]

Christians are still "people of the Book." Our collective story and the very essence of our faith are still found within its pages. It points us to Jesus, "the author and perfecter of our faith" (Heb 12:2). It describes the people we are and guides us to the people we are to become.

13. Williams, *Being Christian*, 21–22.

Chapter 11

Q. *What is the Church?*

A. *The Church is the community of the New Covenant.*

Q. *Why is the church described as one?*

A. *The Church is one, because it is one Body, under one Head, our Lord Jesus Christ.*

Q. *What is the mission of the Church?*

A. *The mission of the Church is to restore all people to unity with God and each other in Christ.*

The Body of Christ

I GREW UP IN Ballard, a heavily Scandinavian area of Seattle at the time. The church my family attended was the merger of an old Norwegian church and an old Swedish church. Whereas services in the original churches had been in Norwegian and Swedish, respectively, they now were in English to accommodate both groups of people as well as second- and third-generation congregants who spoke neither Norwegian nor Swedish. We had a wonderful grandfatherly pastor. He wasn't a dynamic or energetic preacher, but he was good-natured and kind and wonderful at pastoral care. Several families had been in the church for years, some connected through marriage to other members, and the church community had a warm, extended-family kind of feel to it.

Looking back, I credit this community of believers for being my saving grace during my teen years. I was not popular in school, but I had many friends in the church youth group and caring adults who took an interest in me and my brothers. I never had to be coerced into going to youth group on Sunday night or participating in church events. Church was a welcoming, safe place, and even in high school it was where I most often wanted to be.

It wasn't perfect. I remember when some ladies of the church were buzzing when an African American woman, the daughter-in-law of one older (white) couple, came to church with her biracial children, although I know they were treated very civilly. Another tiny scandal occurred when one of the girls in our youth group was rumored to date a boy who was black. I didn't think much about the gossip at the time; it was years before I developed any real sensitivity to racial discrimination. Our church, like our area of Seattle, was a very Caucasian place.

The pulpit stood in the center of the dais and behind it, the choir loft. Behind the choir loft was a large blank wall made of concrete blocks painted light green. There was talk of putting a cross on it, but a few objected, thinking it smacked too much of Catholicism.

I certainly became familiar with the Bible. I wouldn't think of coming to church without my Bible and, like everyone else, it was always open for reference during sermons and Sunday School lessons. I memorized many Bible verses. We acknowledged Jesus as our Savior and Lord, and we were challenged to live exemplary Christian lives.

It wasn't until years later that I became aware of the church's ability to inspire as well as encourage and challenge. On my first visit to St. Aldate's Church in Oxford, during a post-graduate year in England, I was incredibly moved by the sense of sacred space, the inspiring hymns by English composers, and the beautiful words of the liturgy. I was hooked. If my family were to ask why I left the Evangelical church to become an Episcopalian (close to apostasy in their minds, I suspect), I would answer that I have never been more deeply moved or felt closer to God than I have in an Anglican liturgical service.

Medieval architects understood the importance of inspiration. The soaring naves were designed to lift one's eyes to heaven. The purpose of stained-glass windows was to create a sort of light from heaven, evoking in the sacred space the presence of God. They also served to illustrate biblical stories to congregants who were illiterate.[1]

My childhood piano teacher told me that the most inspiring music in the world was written for the church, and I'd have to agree. Although I've heard it many times, the Sanctus from Fauré's Requiem still never fails to send chills up my spine. The most thrilling musical experiences I've ever had were singing in the choir in performances of Bach's St. John Passion, St. Matthew Passion, and the B Minor Mass. I can easily choke up singing Herbert Howell's hymn "All My Hope on God Is Founded" or hearing Hubert Parry's majestic "I Was Glad."

However, it would be wrong to think of the church just in terms of inspiring music or architecture or stained glass or even liturgy. (On the other end of the liturgical spectrum, it would be wrong to think of church in terms of praise bands, theater lighting, and padded pews.) Because the church is the people who gather together to pray, consider Jesus's teaching, and live out his commandments. As the Catechism says, "The Church is the community of the New Covenant." These communities also meet in homes, school gymnasiums, and empty storefronts. They receive their inspiration from the study of Scripture, hearing others talk about their faith, and the mutual encouragement members give each other through the ups and downs of their spiritual journey.

1. Carter, "9 Things," para. 9.

The word "church" has its origins in the word *kyrike,* meaning "belonging to the Lord."[2] In his letter to the church at Corinth, Paul describes the community of early Christians as "the body of Christ." He writes, "Now you are the body of Christ, and each one of you is a part of it" (1 Cor 12:27).[3] He continues to explain that different members of the community will have different roles because of their different gifts, just as the many parts of the body all have different functions. All are important to the functioning of the whole. As Paul writes in his letter to the church in Corinth, "Just as a body, though one, has many parts, but all its many parts form one body, so it is with Christ. For we were all baptized by one Spirit so as to form one body—whether Jews or Gentiles, slave or free—and we were all given the one Spirit to drink. Even so the body is not made up of one part but of many" (1 Cor 12:12–14).

Saint Benedict felt very strongly about the importance of a stable faith-centered community. He had no use for *sarabaites,* those calling themselves monks who wandered from place to place, not adhering to any rule of life. Nor did he approve of *gyrovagues,* who moved from community to community, not committing to any. Joan Chittister put it this way:

> Modern society has the idea that if you want to live a truly spiritual life, you have to leave life as we know it and go away by yourself and "contemplate," and that if you do, you will get holy. It is a fascinating although mislead-ing thought. The Rule of Benedict says that if you want to be holy, stay where you are in the human community and learn from it. Learn patience. Learn wisdom. Learn unselfishness. Learn love.[4]

The church is the community in which we practice those gifts of the Spirit we can only learn by being with others. It is the place where we hone our faith by rubbing up against others' sometimes differing beliefs and difficult behavior. As we share the ups and

2. Steinke, *Your Church Family,* 61.

3. New International Version—UK.

4. Chittester, *Rule of Benedict,* 33.

downs of our spiritual journey, we are encouraged and challenged by our brothers and sisters in Christ.

Diana Butler Bass would say that the church is not only a community, but it is also a "communion," a set of relationships making up a mode of being.[5] She goes on to write, "This sort of belonging insists that the community must be a dynamic, ongoing love, a passionate romance between the divine and the mundane that seduces us into an intimate relationship with God, our neighbors, and our own deepest self."

Chapter 12

Q. Who are the ministers of the Church?

*A. The ministers of the Church are lay persons,
bishops, priests, and deacons.*

Q. What is the ministry of the laity?

*A. The ministry of lay persons is to represent
Christ and his Church; to bear witness to
him wherever they may be; and, according
to the gifts given them, to carry on Christ's
work of reconciliation in the world; and
to take their place in the life, worship, and
governance of the Church.*

The Call to Ministry

MINISTER COMES FROM THE Old French word *menistre* and from
Latin *minister*, meaning servant, as in valet or one who serves
tables. What then is *ministry*? Every minister has a different answer to that question related to their different callings, and there
are many different models appropriate to specific roles and those
being served: chaplaincy vs. small pastor-centered parish vs. large
program-centered church. (It does not usually involve serving

tables.) To most people, the word *minister* suggests an ordained clergy person, although the Book of Common Prayer identifies as ministers all who represent Christ and his church.

The topic of priests is mentioned quite a few times in the Hebrew Scriptures, although not a lot is said about their role. The book of Genesis mentions that King Melchizedek of Salem, a "priest of God Most High," brought out bread and wine as part of worship, and Leviticus describes explicitly what priests are to do with animal sacrifices and grain offerings. The first ordination is mentioned in the book of Exodus where God tells Moses to consecrate Aaron and his sons as priests. The design of their vestments and the parts of the ordination ceremony are described in great detail (Exod 28–29).

Chapter 6 of Acts introduces the act of ordination in the early church in response to a problem within the community of believers. Those early followers of the Way shared all things in common, but the Hellenists among them complained that some of their widows were being neglected in the daily distribution of food. So the leaders (the twelve apostles) called together the whole community and suggested that they select from among them seven men of good standing, "full of the Spirit and of wisdom" (Acts 6:5), whom they could appoint to this task of ministering to the needs of individuals within the community. They chose first Stephen and then six others (Philip, Prochorus, Nicanor, Timon, Parmenas, and Nicolaus) as *deacons*. The men stood before the apostles, who prayed and laid hands on them. Interestingly, the ordination of priests is not mentioned in the New Testament at all, although Paul does mention pastors, evangelists, and prophets. The role of priest as Christians understand it today is a holdover from ancient Jewish faith.

Having several friends who are priests and a brother who is an ordained minister, I know that the role of clergy is not easy. One priest friend tells me that one of the biggest challenges he has experienced is meeting others' expectations as to what his ministry should be. Many priests will tell you that several aspects of leading a church are not taught in seminary, such as models of leadership, budgets, handling the emotional stress of the job, and tending to one's own emotional and spiritual life. Parishioners and dioceses vary widely in their support of their priests.

On the other hand, the best part of being a priest, I was told, is the privilege of being present to people during the best and worst moments of their life and bringing spiritual insight to those moments. Priests who live into their calling love the challenge of growing, learning, solving new problems—personally and professionally—and leading a congregation to develop and thrive as a Christian community.

At the 1976 General Convention of the Episcopal Church, the term *total ministry* came into use. Total ministry is the development of ministry among the whole church, lay and ordained, in all areas of life.[1] Martin Luther proposed the idea of the priesthood of all believers, asserting the ministry of all members of the church in their collective mission to the world.[2] Prior to the sixteenth century, ministry was pretty much restricted to clerics, those educated and ordained for their authoritative role. The church was divided into clergy and clients, "those who *did* ministry and those who were *done to*" as Urban Holmes put it.[3]

When Barbara Brown Taylor told her bishop that she wanted to be ordained a priest, he responded, "Think hard before you do this. Right now, you have the broadest ministry imaginable. As a layperson, you can serve God no matter what you do for a living, and you can reach out to people who will never set foot inside a church. Once you are ordained, that is going to change."[4]

I was unprepared for my calling to the ministry of the laity. Although I had sung in the cathedral choir and occasionally read one of the Sunday Scripture lessons, I did not feel like much of a player. I didn't go out of my way to serve God, nor did I have a regular prayer practice. I did, however, want to go deeper in my faith. One January, I joined an intentional community of thoughtful,

1. "Total Ministry," para. 1.
2. "Ministry," para. 3.
3. Holmes, *Spirituality for Ministry*, 30.
4. Taylor, *Leaving Church*, 40.

compassionate people dedicated to the Benedictine principle of *ora et labora* (prayer and work), *labora* including Christian service to others. I had come to understand that faith was probably less about what I thought I believed and more about the faith that I practiced.

One Sunday, the dean of cathedral I attended talked about the cathedral's food ministry in the Sunday announcements and offered an invitation to "come have lunch with us on Wednesday." I immediately said to myself, *That would be good, but no thanks. I'm sure I have something more important to do.* I knew that the food ministry catered to people I would usually make a point of avoiding if I saw them on the street. Through some self-awareness and most probably the work of the Holy Spirit, I quickly realized that avoidance was a barrier I needed to deal with. I was reminded of Scripture I previously had not paid much attention to and the many references in the Hebrew Scriptures and New Testament about the poor and God's attitude toward the poor. I had heard about "Matthew 25 Christians," the ones who took Christ's teachings seriously, such those in the parable of the king who sorts the "sheep" from the "goats":

> The righteous will answer him, "Lord, when did we see you hungry, and feed you, or thirsty, and give you something to drink? And when did we see you a stranger, and invite you in, or naked, and clothe you? When did we see you sick, or in prison, and come to you?" The King will answer and say to them, "Truly I say to you, to the extent that you did it to one of these brothers of mine, even the least of them, you did it to me." (Matt 25:37–40)

So the following week I showed up on Wednesday, and was greeted at the door by an old-timer named Fred who pointed me to a table with five other men. I was somewhat nervous about this, wondering what I would say to men that I had nothing in common with. Surprisingly, the conversation was free-flowing and pleasant. And I was very impressed with the good food and the gracious service by the volunteers. I decided I needed to come back as a volunteer, and that's what I did. In this case, my ministry did relate to the word's etymology: I became one of the Wednesday table servers and also took my turn at bussing as guests finished their meals and we put down new place settings for others.

I wasn't practiced in seeing the divine in others, but over the next few weeks and months, I worked on that. I learned from my Wednesday meal experience that it isn't hard to see the Christ in others when you look for the Christ in others. Over the years of serving at the Wednesday lunch I got to know some good-humored, intelligent, loving people among our guests, and my life is richer for it. Learning to love less fortunate neighbors opened my heart in ways that I never thought possible.

Several years later, on a trip to Italy, I found myself standing in San Luigi dei Francesi Church in Rome, looking at a painting by Caravaggio, *La Vocazione di San Matteo* (*The Calling of Saint Matthew*). In the painting, Matthew, the tax collector, sits at a table in the customs house, counting coins with two other men as two well-dressed boys sit with them, looking on. The light from a high window bathes their faces as the men turn toward the interruption at the entrance to the room. At the door, the figure of Jesus, partially silhouetted by the light behind him and partially obscured by Saint Peter standing in front of him, points toward Matthew. Matthew points a finger at himself and a quizzical look crosses his face, as if he's saying, "Who, me?" The painting represents a man caught between two worlds and an encounter that begins a personal transformation.

What historians know about Caravaggio today is largely known from his police files. He was a troublemaker and brawler and was banished from Rome for killing another man in an argument over a tennis match. However, he was drawn to painting saints and religious scenes, sometimes using notorious prostitutes as models. People either loved or hated his art based on how they felt about his portrayal of religious figures as common people.

What resonated with me (and, I think, must have resonated with Caravaggio) was the unexpected nature of Christ's call, for Matthew as well as myself. Matthew was a tax collector, a group despised by the Jews for their role in working for the occupying force and taking additional fees for themselves. I came to lay ministry as a gay man who loved martinis, Broadway shows, and jazz clubs—no one's idea of a holy person. Rachel Held Evans wrote that what is most annoying and beautiful about the Holy Spirit is that it has this habit of showing up in all the wrong places and among all the wrong people.[5] However, when Christ comes to us, we are compelled to look up from what we are doing, listen with the ear of our heart, and follow.

Lisa Fischbeck asks, "What if we ordained the laity?" Upon her ordination, she wondered what the church would be like—indeed, what the world would be like—if we did something comparable for laity who are also called by God to ministry in the world.

> What if we set apart, prayed over, laid hands upon, sent forth, gave gifts and had a cake, for the teacher, the nurse, the lawyer, the retiree, the shop keeper, the stay-at-home parent, the social worker, the person living with a disability? What if we encouraged them to invite their family, friends, colleagues and neighbors to the celebration? What if we gave the church a chance to say that we believe this person is called to this ministry and that we will do all in their power to support them in it?[6]

She concludes that commissioning the laity for their ministry in the world can help us more fully to realize and to make known that their ministry is essential to the work of the kingdom of God.

> *If you cannot preach like Peter,*
> *If you cannot pray like Paul,*
> *You can tell the love of Jesus,*
> *And say, "He died for all."*[7]

---

5. Evans, *Searching for Sunday*, 197.

6. Fischbeck, "Called to Ministry," para. 2.

7. African American spiritual, "Balm in Gilead."

Chapter 13

Q. What is prayer?

A. Prayer is responding to God, by thought and by deeds, with or without words.

Q. What are the principal kinds of prayer?

A. The principal kinds of prayer are adoration, praise, thanksgiving, penitence, oblation, intercession, and petition.

Learning to Pray

MY MEMORY OF IT is hazy, happening so many years ago. I don't remember where I parked my little purple moped—someplace along St. Aldate's or Pembroke Street. I was probably excited and a little nervous as I took off my helmet and entered the doors to St. Aldate's Church, a popular church with Oxford University students. My friend Dave, who previously had lived in Oxford for a year, suggested that I really had to check it out. The building itself was a sooty old Gothic structure, the nave and chancel constructed in the twelfth-century and comprising the central part of the building as it now stands, although the building I entered had been extended as the church grew. I thrilled at the enthusiastic singing of old Anglican hymns by the full-throated voices of the mostly student congregation, accompanied masterfully by the musician on the bench of the old pipe organ. The order of service, prayers, and responses were found in a little, green, paperback booklet in the pew rack.

Discovering liturgical worship was a revelation to me. It was here in this Anglican church that I first attempted prayer with others from a prayer book, marveling at the thoughtful, beautiful words—almost poetry—expressing profound sentiments in words I never could have put together myself. Only then, as an adult in my late twenties, did I realize I could have a heartfelt conversation with God using someone else's words.

I first learned to pray around the dinner table, a routine I remember from my earliest memories. At first either my mom or dad asked God's blessing for the food, using their own words, but tending to say nearly the same things every night. My mom, the more ardent evangelical, prayed more fervently, her voice attempting to reflect real gratitude, whether or not she was really feeling it after dealing with five noisy boys all day. My dad, the engineer, prayed in a more measured way, always clearing his throat before he began, carefully choosing the right words, and expressing them in a matter-of-fact manner.

As we got old enough, we boys took turns offering the evening's grace. To begin with, our prayers were short and to the point: "Dear God, thank you for this food. In Jesus's name, amen." As we heard others pray in church, often with long, loquacious intercessions, we too would attempt to include more. Our prayers might not only address the food, but a sick friend, the sun and the flowers, and anything else that would pop into our heads. Then, by adolescence, impatient at waiting for others and anxious to get to the food, they became more concise again, along the lines of, "Dear God, thank you for this food, in Jesus's name, amen."

Dad always prayed over the meal at family gatherings—Thanksgiving, Christmas, and occasionally other holidays—in his measured but sincere way. If my Aunt Helen was present (which she almost always was), she would always add this coda: "And bless the hands that have prepared it."

Our prayer education continued in other ways as well. Every evening, after every dinner and before dessert, Dad led the family in evening devotions, reading a bit of Scripture or a chapter from a devotional book, and praying together. We also memorized Scripture together: Luke 2 (the story of Christ's birth) which we continued to recite every Christmas for many years, Ps 1, Ps 100, Ps 91, the first chapter of John's Gospel. This routine of dinner table worship taught us that faith wasn't just a Sunday thing, but something we practiced in everyday life. During our post-dinner prayer time, Dad would say the first prayer, and Mom would close in prayer, but each of us were invited to add our own prayers, and we all did, not wanting to be outdone by our brothers. We modeled the prayers we heard in church. We prayed for our relatives, missionaries our church supported, sick acquaintances, and God's protection and guidance for upcoming events. And we thanked God for our blessings, although, depending on our moods at the time, these were sometimes harder to generate.

I don't remember exactly when the habit of daily prayer went away, but sometime during my twenties it did. That's not to say I never prayed. When my heart was unexpectedly touched, I directed my gratitude toward God, and when I needed something from God, I was still inclined to offer a brief petition. However, that habit of greeting God in the morning, setting aside a quiet time for prayer during the day, and saying goodnight to God as I lay my head on the pillow, giving thanks for the blessings of the day, were no longer part of my daily routine. Saying a grace before a meal in a restaurant seemed to me to be a little like the proud Pharisee praying on the street corner that Jesus talked about, and so I dropped that practice. Which led me to not bothering to pray before meals when I was alone at home either.

So, discovering and praying with others the beautiful words in the English prayer book at St. Aldate's Church in Oxford made me take a fresh look at prayer, where I was frequently moved by the sentiments expressed in the little prayer book and the fact that I was collectively expressing those sentiments aloud with my brothers and sisters in Christ. To this day I deeply love hearing the Prayer for Purity at the beginning of the service ("to you all hearts are open, all desires known . . .") and saying the thanksgiving at the end ("you have graciously accepted us as living members of your Son our Savior Jesus Christ . . .").

It was in the Episcopal church a few years later that I learned there were short prayer services for various times of the day. As a new Episcopalian at another popular student church in Tempe, Arizona, where I was doing graduate work, I was soon put to work as a lector, occasionally leading the service of Morning Prayer. I later learned about Noon Prayer, Evening Prayer, and Compline, the service meant to be said before you lay your head down at night. One of my very favorite prayers comes from this service: "Keep watch, dear Lord, with those who work and watch and weep this night . . ." For most of the church's history, Christians didn't understand prayer as a means of self-expression or a personal conversation with the divine, but rather as a corporate way of approaching God through the Divine Office.[1]

It was at an Episcopal prayer retreat, in New York state years later, that I learned about *lectio divina*, praying the Scriptures. Where my previous experience with prayer was largely comprised of talking to God (verbalizing petitions and intercessions from a heart God could already read very well), *lectio divina* presented the opportunity to *listen* as God spoke to me through Scripture. The routine began with reading to identify a word, phrase, or idea that resonated. Contemplation expanded with each repeated reading, including answering the question *What is God saying to me through this passage?*

In 2009, after a period of spiritual sleepwalking, I joined an intentional community that studied the Rule of St. Benedict and together liked to read books by Benedictine authors. My growing interest in things monastic led me to visit a monastery in northern New Mexico that observed "the Divine Office," or seven prayer services throughout the day, starting with Vigils at four o'clock in

1. Warren, *Prayer in the Night*, 8.

the morning. I gamely participated as best I could, rousing myself at 3:45 to splash some water on my face, dress, and take the seven-minute brisk walk to the chapel, using my flashlight to see my way along the gravel road.

I learned some wonderful things by dwelling amongst the monks for several days. I discovered, first, that chanting the psalms is very effective in making certain phrases and verses stick in your head. I remember taking an afternoon hike to see more of the canyon, chanting "Answer me, O God, defender of my cause; You set me free when I am hard-pressed . . ." from a psalm we had chanted earlier in the day. Also, observing the Daily Office seven times a day was very conducive to being in a prayerful state of mind all day. This doesn't mean I was always consciously praying, but I was aware of a heightened state of mindfulness and hypersensitivity to God's presence. Finally, I learned the value of simplicity and silence. Removing the distractions in life made room for other things in my consciousness and spirit. The monks live a life devoted to prayer and work (*ora et labora*), although God's most important work (*opus dei*) is prayer.

It was also as a Benedictine enthusiast that I learned about contemplative prayer which, according to Cynthia Bourgeault, "is simply a wordless, trusting opening of self to the divine presence."[2] Although popularized in the 1970s, it has an ancient origin, going back to the Desert Mothers and Fathers who were the first to practice it, as well as the early Benedictines. The practice was documented and preserved for the future in a book entitled *The Cloud of Unknowing* by an anonymous fourteenth-century author, probably a British monk, who wrote the text in Middle English. The point of contemplative prayer is, according to Thomas Keating, to take a brief vacation from yourself and be totally open to God. Cynthia Bourgeault says the first step "is simply to pull the plug on that constant self-reflexive activity of the mind."[3] I was discouraged by my first attempts at contemplative prayer and soon gave it up. I returned to it again when I realized that one's mind

2. Bourgeault, *Centering Prayer*, 5.
3. Bourgeault, *Centering Prayer*, 16.

was meant to be active and I learned to notice my mind's distract-ibility without judgment, patiently and persistently releasing those thoughts and returning to a focus on God's presence.

I also came to realize that contemplation was a *grace*, a gift from God. Michael Casey wrote, "In contemplative prayer God ceases to be the object of our prayer, but becomes its subject. God is the one who prays in us . . . having the mind of Christ, to use Saint Paul's phrase."[4] I haven't yet reached that empty, quiet place where I experience total surrender in prayer, but I hold to the promise as Cynthia Bourgeault stated it: "Every time you are willing to release a thought, to perform the gesture of self-emptying, this gesture is patterned and strengthened within you."[5]

In learning contemplative prayer, I certainly have not aban-doned other modes of prayer. Nothing will replace for me the thrill and comfort of praying in a collective way the words and ideas beautifully expressed in the liturgy. I still include petitions (prayers for myself) and intercessions (prayers for others) in my devotional time, but it's less about thinking I might change God's mind about things and more along the lines of "Thy will be done on earth as it is in heaven." The proclamations of praise in the Daily Office, both in the psalms and the prayers, are not done to stroke God's ego, but more to inspire in us a spirit of gratitude that helps us reframe all the events—good and bad—in our lives.

Just as contemplation is a gift from God, so the Holy Spirit helps us in other forms of prayer as well. As it says in Paul's letter to the Romans, "Likewise the Spirit helps us in our weakness; for we do not know how to pray as we ought, but that very Spirit inter-cedes with sighs too deep for words. And God, who searches the heart, knows what is the mind of the Spirit, because the Spirit in-tercedes for the saints according to the will of God" (Rom 8:26–27).

I think of prayer as a way of sustaining a valued relationship. Communication is vital in maintaining our human relationships. Would it not be the same for maintaining our relationship with God? Interactions don't always have to be wonderful experiences;

4. Casey, *Grace*, 120.

5. Casey, *Grace*, 122.

in fact, some of them may be painful or mundane. Similarly, we come to God as we are—happy, weary, cranky, or bored—and our prayer in all its forms is a way of keeping alive our relationship with God. As Tish Harrison Warren writes, "Faith, I've come to believe, is more craft than feeling. And prayer is our chief practice in the craft."[6] She also points out that a regular prayer practice does not make us float from spiritual bliss to spiritual bliss uninterrupted, but it does correct our vision over time.[7] My hope is that, in time, prayer will begin to take shape as a magnetic center within me, and that my petty concerns, grievances, daydreams, and preoccupations will diminish, overcome by the power of God's presence and love.

6. Warren, *Prayer in the Night*, 8.
7. Warren, *Prayer in the Night*, 64.

Chapter 14

Q. *What are the sacraments?*

A. *The sacraments are outward and visible signs of inward and spiritual grace, given by Christ as sure and certain means by which we receive that grace.*

Q. *What is Holy Baptism?*

A. *Holy Baptism is the sacrament by which God adopts us as his children and makes us member of Christ's Body, the Church, and inheritors of the kingdom of God.*

Marked as Christ's Own

NOT EVERYONE REMEMBERS THEIR baptism. I do.

It was the summer I turned seventeen and I decided that the next step in my life of faith should be to get baptized. I was raised in a church tradition in which baptism was a decision the mature (or, in my case, gradually maturing) Christian made for themselves. It took place in a lake at a church camp near Olympia,

Washington. My parents, people in my church family, and others who had come to family camp in August stood on the bank of the lake. After a prayer, a few words from the officiating pastor, and probably a hymn sung *a cappella* in four-part harmony, I waded into cool waist-deep water when it was my turn to be immersed. The pastor said a short prayer for me, then with one hand on the back of my neck and the other around my hands held tightly on my chest, he tipped me back with the words, "In the name of the Father, the Son, and the Holy Spirit." I held my breath, bent my knees as instructed, and let the water envelop me. A person waited for me on the bank with a towel when it was all over, and I walked up the bank to sit with my friends in the grass.

It wasn't a highly emotional experience for me, like some spiritual experiences I've had, but I do remember having a feeling of satisfaction and accomplishment, knowing it was an important spiritual milestone. I had publicly declared my faith and commitment to Christ in front of friends and strangers. I didn't understand the word "sacrament" at the time, but I did have a sense of that "inward and spiritual grace." I knew I had been obedient to the Scripture's teaching and the Holy Spirit's leading.

Baptism has a long history. Water rituals, including baptisms, were fairly common throughout the ancient Near East.[1] The Jews believed water had the power to transport a person or object from unclean to clean, from profane to holy. Gentile converts to Judaism would take a ceremonial bath to rid themselves of their former identity and become part of their chosen tribe. The Bible contains examples of many ablutionary practices. After hearing the good news of Christ from the apostle Philip, the Ethiopian eunuch sees water and says, "What's to prevent me from being baptized?" (Acts 8:38).

Marcus Borg wrote that sacred rituals are reenactments or embodiments of sacred story.[2] Through ritual, one relives the story. Whereas communion is a reenactment of the Last Supper, Jesus's Passover supper with his disciples the night before his

1. Aslan, *Zealot*, 83–86.
2. Borg, *God We Never Knew*, 117.

crucifixion, baptism is a little different. It is not just a reminder of Jesus's baptism in the Jordan River, but also a symbolic representation of his death, burial, and resurrection. Rowan Williams says that, from the very beginning, the baptism ritual was associated with the idea of going down into the darkness of Jesus's suffering and death, "being 'swamped' by the reality of what Jesus endured."[3] But, as a priest friend reminded me, it doesn't leave us submerged in the swamp. Baptism also carries with it the reality of being risen to new life, a life in which God adopts us as his children and makes us member of Christ's body, the church.

Today, baptisms very often are a moving experience for me, and I realize that it is a passage of significance for the whole church, the assembled body of Christ, not just for the one being baptized or their parents. After families, standing together in front of their church family, have made their promises to see that the child they present will be brought up in the Christian life, help their child to grow into the full stature of Christ, renounce the evil powers of this world, and turn to Jesus Christ as their Savior, the congregation, with a loud "We will," also vows to support the newly baptized in their life in Christ. Indeed, raising a child in a life of faith "takes a village"—or at least a church community. I may have to wipe a tear away when the priest makes the sign of the cross with oil on the child's forehead, saying "marked as Christ's own forever."

Scott Cormode recalls a routine the pastor of his Connecticut church "followed whenever she baptized a child. After the ceremony, she took the child in her arms and walked her through the congregation, saying 'This is <child's name>. She belongs to God. And she belongs to us.'"[4]

In the Episcopal church, baptism also includes the whole congregation renewing their baptismal covenant, starting with the Apostles Creed. Then follow promises to continue in the apostles' teaching and fellowship; participate in communion and prayer; persevere in resisting evil, and, when we fail (as we will), repent; proclaim by word and example the good news; seek and serve

---

3. Williams, *Being Christian*, 1–2.

4. Cormode, "Baptism Stories," para. 4.

Christ in all persons and love our neighbor as ourself; strive for justice and peace; and respect the dignity of every human being. Tall orders, to which we humbly respond, "I will, with God's help." In our church, after the baptisms, the rite ends with the *asperges* in which the assisting clergy walk down the aisles sprinkling the congregants with the words "Recall the waters of your baptism . . ."

I like the fact that our baptism isn't just an experience we leave behind us after our own is done. It is an experience we relive and promises we renew every time we join with other Christians to celebrate a baptism. It gives us a chance to remember who we are and to whom we belong, that we are marked as Christ's own forever. It gives us a chance to promise again to continue in Christian practices, including loving our neighbor as ourselves. It puts us again "in the depths"[5] with Jesus.

---

5. Williams, *Being Christian*, 5.

Chapter 15

Q. What is the Holy Eucharist?

A. The Holy Eucharist is the sacrament commended by Christ for the continual remembrance of his life, death, and resurrection, until his coming again.

Food for the Traveler

HOLY EUCHARIST IS A ceremonial reenactment of that last supper that Christ had with his disciples just prior to his betrayal, arrest, and crucifixion. Bruce Chilton claims that the Last Supper was actually a series of table fellowships that Jesus had with his disciples involving wine and bread after the disruptive event in the temple in which Jesus overturned the money changers' tables.[1] Jesus celebrated these meals as a foretaste of the kingdom. According to Chilton, the new scandalous dimension to the meals, probably causing Judas to inform on Jesus, were the words "This is my flesh," and "This is my blood." Touching dead flesh and, certainly, eating human flesh was abhorrent to Jews, as it would be to many of us today.

1. Chilton, *Pure Kingdom*, 123–25.

According to the Book of Common Prayer, the Holy Eucharist is for the continual remembrance of Christ's life, death, and resurrection. Cynthia Bourgeault maintains that its authors didn't get that quite right. The sharing of bread and wine is not primarily a memorial meal, but rather a spiritual practice in which Jesus is as present now as he was then. Jesus was intent upon establishing a living connection, an open energetic channel that would allow him to remain in communion within the hearts of his beloved followers. "I in you and you in me so that we all may be one." [2]

In many churches, baptism and right belief are requirements for coming to the Lord's table. However, Peter Marty and others offer the suggestion that maybe the grace experienced in the sacrament precedes belief, rather than the other way around. "Maybe it's time we start seeing the Eucharist as Christ doling out thick love to all God's people," writes Marty, "whether their belief is sturdy, shaky, or very much unformed."[3]

Bourgeault tells the story of going to her first communion entirely by chance, primarily to hear a well-known boy choir performing in the service.[4] Following an usher's direction she found herself inadvertently in a communion line. Terrified, she awkwardly took the wafer and the cup and rose from the altar rail thinking, "Well, that's that." About two thirds of the way back to her pew she quietly realized that something utterly real and strangely compelling had entered her life that day.

In her wonderful book, *Take This Bread*, Sara Miles tells the story of her first visit to Saint Gregory of Nyssa church in San Francisco, primarily out of curiosity.[5] Following everyone else, she was swept forward around the altar, ate a piece of bread, took a sip of wine, and left forever changed. She writes, "Holy communion knocked me upside down and forced me to deal with the impossible reality of God."

2. Bourgeault, *Wisdom Jesus*, 186–87.

3. Marty, "Who Is Welcome?," para. 8.

4. Bourgeault, *Wisdom Jesus*, 184.

5. Miles, *Take This Bread*.

I was raised in a church that, in order to preserve communion as a special event, offered it only three or four times a year. Much was made of the fact that this rite was only for those that had accepted Jesus as their Savior, and there was teaching about the peril of eating and drinking unworthily (1 Cor 11:27). I was never glad that the Sunday morning service included communion because it added fifteen or twenty minutes to the length of the service and the pastor was never inclined to shorten his sermon because of it.

The communion rite was very somber and included Scripture reading from the account of the Last Supper, a gospel hymn such as "The Old Rugged Cross" or "Nothing but the Blood of Jesus," that was sung way too slowly, and a long prayer. We remained seated as silver plates were passed down each row by the ushers and from which we took a tiny, square, cracker-like wafer. We held these until the pastor said a prayer of thanksgiving for the bread and we ingested it together. Then came the round silver dish with holes designed to hold the tiny shot glasses with grape juice. After another prayer for the "wine," we all tossed it back.

I thought of it as a Christian duty, nothing I looked forward to or took anything away from. It never touched my heart or impressed me as something that I particularly needed on my Christian path.

I experienced something far different when I walked into St. Aldate's Church for the first time during the year I studied abroad in England. It was my first real experience of Anglican liturgy, my first experience kneeling during prayer, my first experience in going forward to an altar rail for communion. I was moved by the words from the prayer book, the wonderful old Anglican hymns, and the whole spirit of the place. When I came forward for Eucharist, overcoming my awkwardness at doing something a new way, I knew immediately as I knelt at the altar rail that I had come to partake. A wafer was placed in my palm, and a cup was lifted to my lips. I returned to my pew and knelt in prayer while tears ran down my cheeks. I knew that I had left something of myself at the altar rail and had received something life-giving in return. I knew I was welcome; I knew I was home.

Today I am often moved during the Eucharist. Sometimes the stimulus is the personal hunger or intention I bring to the altar, but more often it is the experience of joining with the community in a sacred act. Coming from a doctrinal church that encouraged conformity of belief, the most disconcerting thing to me when I first joined the Episcopal Church was learning that my fellow parishioners held such a wide range of faith beliefs, some—to my evangelical mind—bordering on the heretical. Now it is one of the things I appreciate most: that God welcomes all of us around God's table, regardless of where we are on our spiritual journey or how orthodox or unorthodox our understanding. Christ gives of himself to each of us, and each of us takes away the nourishment we need. My first priest in the Episcopal Church, Father Frank, made the point that every Sunday we have an "altar call." And each Sunday, when I go forward for Communion, my intention is to open my heart to Christ's presence, ingest him again into my life and my being, and rededicate myself to his service.

Chapter 16

Q. *What is the Christian hope?*

A. *The Christian hope is to live with confidence in newness and fullness of life, and to await the coming of Christ in glory, and the completion of God's purpose for the world.*

Q. *What do we mean by heaven and hell?*

A. *By heaven, we mean eternal life in our enjoyment of God; by hell, we mean eternal death in our rejection of God.*

Heaven and Hell

I SUSPECT THAT MANY of my friends think it's somewhat quaint that I believe in heaven and hell. I was raised to believe in heaven and hell, although my ideas about them as a child were quite different than how I think of them today. Like many people, my childhood images of heaven were based on biblical metaphors: streets of gold, gates of pearl, angels and such floating around God's throne. I didn't grow up in a hellfire-and-brimstone church, so I didn't have very salient images of hell, although I certainly learned it was a place where I didn't want to go. In my child's mind it was a vague place that was way too dark and way too hot, where one was surrounded by very unpleasant people who were always sweating.

Belief in heaven appears to be ancient and cross-cultural. These beliefs center around both the physical characteristics of heaven as a place and the beings that get to live there. The ancient Mesopotamians thought of heaven as a series of domes in the sky, covering a flat earth, each dome made of a different kind of precious stone. Ordinary mortals could not go to heaven because it was the abode of the gods alone. The ancient Hittites believed that some deities lived in heaven, while others lived in remote places on Earth, such as mountains, to which humans had little access. In Chinese Confucian traditions, heaven is where ancestors resided and the emperor dynasties received their mandate to rule.

Both the Hebrew Bible and Islamic texts use a plural word for heaven (*šāmayim* and *samāwāt*, respectively) suggesting multiple parts or layers of heaven, including the stars and galaxies, an idea possibly borrowed from the Mesopotamians. The structure of heaven is never fully described in the Hebrew Bible. There is almost no mention of heaven as an afterlife destination for human beings, who are instead described as "resting" in Sheol. The only two possible exceptions are Enoch, who was "taken" by God, and the prophet Elijah, who ascended to heaven in a chariot of fire.

The New Testament, however, is a different matter. The Gospel of Matthew alone has over sixty references to heaven. Jesus mentioned it often, frequently talking about "the kingdom of heaven" and his "Father in heaven." However, Jesus never described its appearance, but spoke of it metaphorically, comparing it to mustard seed, leaven, hidden treasure, a landowner who hires vineyard workers, and a wedding banquet, among others.

The writer of Revelation does give physical descriptions of heaven, aka the city of God, the New Jerusalem. The writer, while "in the Spirit," looks through a door to see someone sitting on a throne with the appearance of jasper and ruby, and a shiny rainbow surrounds the throne. The sounds he hears are of trumpets and angels and elders singing praises to God. He sees other amazing visions, including a woman clothed with the sun and an enormous red dragon with seven heads and ten horns. The walled city is laid out like a square, with twelve gates, three on each side. The foundations of the city walls are decorated with precious stones. The twelve gates were twelve pearls, each gate made of a single pearl, and the main street of the city is paved with gold. The city does not need any light source but God alone.

Then there is Jesus's promise in John 14: "In my Father's house there are many dwelling places. If it were not so, would I have told you that I go to prepare a place for you?" Clearly, mortals as well as angels have a place in this heaven. In his letter to the Philippians, Paul wrote: "Our citizenship is in heaven, and it is from there that we are expecting a Savior, the Lord Jesus Christ. He will transform the body of our humiliation that it may be conformed to the body of his glory" (Phil 3:20–21a). For many Christians around the world, heaven holds for them the promise of being reunited with those they have loved.

The Landauer Altarpiece by Albrecht Dürer portrays heaven as a rather crowded gathering of believers worshiping the Trinity floating in the upper half of the painting. God the Father is in the center and wearing a crown and dark, royal blue robes. He (in those days God was always perceived as male) holds a crucifix with a living Jesus in front of him, and a dove representing the Holy Spirit hovers overhead. Holding palm branches, a gathering of female saints, led by the Virgin Mary, clusters to the left of the Trinity, and on the right is a crowd of male patriarchs and saints led by John the Baptist. On the level below them, still hovering above the ground, are others in the Church Triumphant, including popes and cardinals, kings, a veiled queen, and commoners in medieval dress, suggesting that all, regardless of status or wealth, can gather around God's throne.

Popular images of heaven tend to feature lots of clouds, people in white robes, and angels with harps. Cinematic representations range from an efficiently run corporate office (*Heaven Can Wait*) to a giant, surreal landscape painting of endless beauty (*What Dreams May Come*) to an urban resort with amazing food (*Defending Your Life*).

In graduate school, I began to think differently about heaven when Father Frank, my first priest upon joining the Episcopal church, said that our spiritual path as Christians was to prepare for the life we would live after death when we are united with Christ. A few years later, I read *The Great Divorce* by C. S. Lewis for the first time. The story begins with the narrator finding himself waiting for a bus in "the grey town," a dismal, nondescript place. He and other passengers get on a celestial bus that takes them to a brilliant and somewhat intimidating land. On getting off the bus, one unhappy passenger begins complaining about the poor management of the place that seems to allow riff-raff to float about there. Another companion, proud of his very moral life, refuses to go farther into the bright land when he encounters a repentant spirit he knew to be a murderer on earth. A bishop decides to turn back when he is challenged to trust as a little child and give up his intellectual pretensions. A fourth visitor cannot give up his cynicism and mistrust. And so on.

Eventually the narrator encounters the author George Macdonald, who explains to him that all "earthly past will have been Heaven to those who are saved. . . . Heaven, once attained, will work backwards and turn even that agony into a glory."[1] Later he continues, "And that is why, at the end of all things, when the sun rises here and the twilight turns to blackness down there, the Blessed will say, 'We have never lived anywhere except in Heaven,' and the Lost, 'We were always in Hell.' And both will speak truly."[2]

Lewis painted for me a vision of heaven as a natural extension of our life here on earth, carrying with it the consequences of choices we make while on earth. If heaven, like God, is eternal, why can't it flow backward as well as forward and be part of our life on earth as well as our experience after death? As Dwight L. Moody once preached, "We talk about heaven being so far away. It is within speaking distance to those who belong there. Heaven is a prepared place for a prepared people."

1. Lewis, *Great Divorce*, 67.
2. Lewis, *Great Divorce*, 68.

In Lewis's story, one of the newly arrived ghosts tells his guiding Spirit that he is interested in meeting distinguished people who are there. The Spirit replies, "Don't you understand? The Glory flows into everyone, and back and from everyone: like light and mirrors. But the light's the thing."[3]

The reason I believe in heaven is that, as many others, I have experienced something of heaven on earth. I might be overcome with emotion, feeling a Divine presence as I sing the words to an especially meaningful hymn in church. I might feel inexpressible joy sitting next to the Chama River in the profound silence and beauty of a New Mexico canyon. I feel chills up and down my spine when hearing the *Sanctus* from Fauré's Requiem. I might think of heaven when I'm sitting around a dinner table with a group of people who love God, love life, and love each other, experiencing a foretaste of a heavenly banquet.

Thin places is a concept that comes from the mystical world of early Celtic Christians, who were deeply connected to the natural world and considered every aspect of life to be infused with the presence of the Divine. To them, thin places were times or settings where the veil between the world and heaven seemed very porous and one could keenly sense the sacred. I can't help but believe that the joy I feel in my thin places foreshadows for me what my soul will experience eternally in life after this life.

I don't maintain a faith practice in the desperate hope of going to heaven someday. I maintain a faith practice because I experience heaven now. I cannot think of a richer and more gratifying way to live.

Those who indulge in bitterness and resentment know a little of what hell is like. Those are emotional states in which it is very hard to experience God's presence. Growing up, hell was described to me not as devils and flames, but as *eternal separation from God*. Thankfully, the dark experiences in my life were relatively short-lived, and God's grace brought me back to a place of peace and connection again. However, I have known people who were not attune to God's grace or receptive to God's love, who did not look

3. Lewis, *Great Divorce*, 82–83.

for the light, who seemed to develop an addiction to anger and un-happiness, and whose final years on earth became for them already a descent into hell.

Sadly, those who have experienced mental illness also know what hell is like. Whereas most can choose whether or not to nurse bitterness and resentment, those with clinical depression have little control over their despair. In these cases one can feel separated from God without actually being separated from God. My prayer for them is that God's grace and love will follow them even there. As the psalm says:

> Where can I go from your spirit?
>   Or where can I flee from your presence?
> If I ascend to heaven, you are there;
>   if I make my bed in Sheol, you are there.
> If I take the wings of the morning
>   and settle at the farthest limits of the sea,
> even there your hand shall lead me,
>   and your right hand shall hold me fast.
> If I say, "Surely the darkness shall cover me,
>   and the light around me become night,"
> even the darkness is not dark to you;
>   the night is as bright as the day,
>   for darkness is as light to you.[4]

I think C. S. Lewis has a point. Just as the dispositions and habits of a child shape the adult he or she will become, so our dispositions and habits of mind are shaping the being we become in the next life. We have dipped our toes into heaven and hell while here on earth and, over time, are plotting a path toward an everlasting life with God or apart from God. We spend time with God now to better welcome God's presence in heaven. We practice love now to increase the love for those we find in Lewis's grey town. And, as in *The Great Divorce*, we will continue to grow and learn and conquer challenges as we move into that brilliant land, ever drawn by a divine light. I look forward to life after death as a place where we continue to experience heaven and, borrowing words

4. Ps 139:7–12.

from Peter's epistle, to "grow in the grace and knowledge of our Lord and Savior Jesus Christ."[5]

> All shall be Amen and Alleluia.
> We shall rest and we shall see.
>   We shall see and we shall know.
> We shall know and we shall love.
>   We shall love and we shall praise.
> Behold our end, which is no end. Amen.

Saint Augustine[6]

5. 2 Peter 3:18

6. As quoted in Tutu, *African Prayer Book,* 33.

Epilogue

Channel's Edge

In January of 2014, Mike and I moved to a condo in North Portland on the banks of the Columbia River's south channel. Our view of the channel included nearby covered boat moorages and clusters of houseboats (or *floating homes* as their owners prefer to call them). The dirt walking path, east across a large undeveloped section of our levee, led to Bridgeton Road, which had the flavor of a resort community, townhouse condominiums on one side of the road with boat and houseboat moorages on the other side, on the channel.

About a quarter of a mile down Bridgeton Road was a little neighborhood hangout called Channel's Edge. The structure was a little house perched on the edge of the bank, which we later learned had started life as a houseboat and, at some point, was hoisted up the bank and supported on its steep location with a foundation of stilts. One of its owners had added a large wooden deck that looked out over the channel. When Bob and Kim bought the place, they originally made it a gift shop, and two of the front rooms had a variety of paintings (of varying quality) and knickknacks with a nautical theme. The house also had a tiny kitchen and, when Bob and Kim decided to do food as well as gifts, they put tables on the deck and in the narrow back room overlooking the deck and the river, what used to be a low-ceilinged back porch. The sign in the window of the front (streetside) door advertised "Live Music on Friday Night."

So, one Friday night, when we had nothing else to do, Mike and I wandered down the levee to the Channel's Edge to check it out. It was a warm but breezy spring evening, and we found the deck full of locals listening to two surprisingly good musicians: a guy named Alan who played a mean guitar and sang the blues, and his bass accompanist. Not finding seats on the deck we went inside and sat at a small two-person table in the back room, with a view of the deck and musicians. The menu was short and the food was simple. We ordered hamburgers, which Bob cooked on the deck grill.

A party atmosphere prevailed. Most of the customers (house-boat people we later learned) seemed to all know each other, and there were lots of hugs and handshakes. People were very friendly to us, as well. Soon the wind got to be too much for the people out-doors and, with the two musicians, they all crowded into the back porch room so the party could continue there. The two musicians quickly set up again at the end of the narrow room and resumed their set.

The music was pulsing, soulful, energizing. One couple, I would guess in their mid-sixties, felt compelled to move with the beat, although only the narrowest of aisles between the café tables provided any space in which to move. They were not deterred. Standing next to us, the man began to sway his shoulders and hips with the music. He looked at the woman. "Are you with me?," he asked.

"I'm with you," she responded. Not sure what to do with her purse, she plopped it on our table, grabbed her beer bottle, and began moving and swaying with him, following him down the narrow aisle toward the musicians, gently bumping into folks seated along the way as their friends cheered them on. After they shimmied up to the musicians, both turned around and shimmied back. The small crowd was totally delighted, all vicariously danc-ing with them. The atmosphere was pure, naked joy.

When we left our newly discovered gathering place, I was still feeling the buzz and elated that Channel's Edge would now be a part of our lives. But—I asked myself, as I sadly tend to do—how does this fit into the life of an aging introvert striving to be a good Benedictine, living simply and centering my life in a new spiritual practice? There was nothing remotely reverent about the evening, and I doubted that many of the dancers and drinkers thought a lot about spiritual things. And yet I felt curiously uplifted from being with them. People had treated us as new friends, and I witnessed love between neighbors and their joy at being together. As I gradually got to know Bob and Kim and others in the community, I learned that strong relationships were formed among the houseboat people, and they looked out for each other in times of need. This was the first of many happy evenings of great music and open, warm-hearted people.

Walking home, my thoughts were filled with gratitude and a new awareness. In particular, two thoughts crossed my mind. The first was something I had recently read: *There is nothing good that does not come from God.* And my second recollection was the ancient hymn we sing on Maundy Thursday: *Ubi caritas et amor, Deus ibi est.* Where charity and love exist, God is there. I only needed to open my eyes and my heart to find God at the neighborhood bar.

> *For everything created by God is good, and nothing is to be rejected, provided it is received with thanksgiving.* (1 Tim 4:4)

Bibliography

Abelard, Peter. "Exposition of the Epistle to the Romans (Excerpt from the Second Book)." Translated by Gerald E. Moffatt. In *A Scholastic Miscellany*, edited and translated by Eugene R. Fairweather, 276–87. Louisville, KY: Westminster John Knox, 1956. https://mis.kp.ac.rw/admin/admin_panel/kp_lms/files/digital/Core%20Books/Theology/Scholastic%20Miscellany%20(Library%20of%20Christian%20Classics).pdf.

Amnesty International. "Death Penalty." https://www.amnesty.org/en/what-we-do/death-penalty/.

Anglican Compass. "Anglican Glossary." https://anglicancompass.com/anglican-glossary/?dir=2&name_directory_startswith=C.

Armentrout, Don S., and Robert Boak Slocum, eds. *An Episcopal Dictionary of the Church: A User-Friendly Reference for Episcopalians*. New York: Church, 2000. https://www.episcopalchurch.org/glossary/catechism/.

Armstrong, Karen. *The Bible*. New York: Atlantic Monthly, 2007.

———. *The Case for God*. New York: Knopf, 2009.

———. *The Great Transformation*. New York: Knopf, 2006.

Aslan, Reza. *Zealot: The Life and Times of Jesus of Nazareth*. New York: Random House, 2013.

Augustine of Hippo. *Confessions*. Translated by Henry Chadwick. New York: Oxford University Press, 1991.

Baker, Lisa Loraine. "What Is the Charismatic Movement?" *Christianity.com,* April 22, 2021. https://www.christianity.com/wiki/christian-terms/what-is-the-charismatic-movement.html.

Bass, Diana Butler. *Christianity after Religion*. New York: HarperOne, 2012.

Borg, Marcus. "Christianity Divided by the Cross." *Patheos* (blog), October 25, 2013. http://www.patheos.com/blogs/marcusborg/2013/10/christianity-divided-by-the-cross/.

———. *The God We Never Knew*. New York: HarperOne, 1997.

———. *Meeting Jesus Again for the First Time*. San Francisco: HarperCollins, 1994.

Bourgeault, Cynthia. *Centering Prayer and Inner Awakening*. Lanham, MD: Cowley, 2004.

———. *The Wisdom Jesus*. Boulder, CO: Shambhala, 2008.

Boyle, Gregory. *Tattoos on the Heart: The Power of Boundless Compassion*. New York: Free Press, 2010.

"A Brief History of Catechisms, and Peter Canisius." *Siris* (blog), December 21, 2011. https://branemrys.blogspot.com/2011/12/brief-history-of-catechisms-and-peter.html.

Brooks, David. *The Second Mountain*. New York: Random House, 2019.

———. *The Social Animal*. New York: Random House, 2011.

Cameron, Julia. *Walking in This World: The Practical Art of Creativity*. New York: Tarcher, 2002.

Carter, Joe. "9 Things You Should Know about Church Architecture." *The Gospel Coalition*, March 24, 2015. https://www.thegospelcoalition.org/article/9-things-you-should-know-about-church-architecture.

Casey, Michael. *Grace: On the Journey to God*. Brewster, MA: Paraclete, 2018.

"Catechism." https://www.newworldencyclopedia.org/entry/Catechism.

Chilton, Bruce. *Pure Kingdom: Jesus' Vision of God*. Grand Rapids, MI: Eerdmans, 1996.

Chittester, Joan D. *The Rule of Benedict: Insights for the Ages*. New York: Crossroad, 2009.

Clement, Olivier. *The Roots of Christian Mysticism*. Translated by T. Berkeley. London: New City Press, 1993.

Connell, J. Clement. "The Propitiatory Element in the Atonement." *Vox Evangelica* 4 (1965) 28–42.

Cormode, Scott. "Baptism Stories." *The Next Faithful Step*, n.d. https://www.fuller.edu/next-faithful-step/classes/cf565/baptism-stories/.

Croft, Steven. "A Very Short History of Catechesis." *Diocese of Oxford* (blog), December 12, 2017. https://blogs.oxford.anglican.org/short-history-catechesis/.

Daily Prayers for All Seasons. New York: Church, 2014.

DeWaal, Esther. *Living with Contradiction*. Harrisburg, PA: Morehouse, 1989.

De Witt, Melissa. "Who People Believe Rules in Heaven Influences Their Beliefs about Who Rules on Earth, Stanford Scholars Find." *Stanford News Service*, January 31, 2020. https://news.stanford.edu/2020/01/31/consequences-perceiving-god-white-man/.

Dietrich, Arne. "The Cognitive Neuroscience of Creativity." *Psychonomic Bulletin & Review* 11 (2004) 1011–26.

Doyle, Leonard J., trans. *St. Benedict's Rule for Monasteries*. Collegeville, MN: Liturgical, 1948.

Durant, Will. *The Life of Greece*. New York: MJF Books, 1939.

Eck, Diana L. *Encountering God: A Spiritual Journey from Bozeman to Banaras*. Boston: Beacon, 1993.

Episcopal Church. *The Book of Common Prayer*. New York: The Church Hymnal Corporation, 1979.

Evangelical Free Church of America. "The EFCA Statement of Faith." https://www.efca.org/sof.

Evans, Rachel Held. *Searching for Sunday*. Nashville, TN: Nelson, 2015.

Fischbeck, Lisa. "Called to Ministry in the World: What If We Ordained the Laity?" *Episcopal Café* (blog), July 13, 2013. https://episcopal.cafe/called_to_ministry_in_the_world_what_if_we_ordained_the_laity/.

Hauerwas, Stanley, and William H. Willimon. *The Holy Spirit*. Nashville, TN: Abingdon, 2015.

Hawthorne, Christopher. "Jorn Utzon Dies at 90; Danish Architect of Sydney Opera House." *Los Angeles Times*, November 30, 2008. https://www.latimes.com/local/obituaries/la-me-utzon30-2008nov30-story.html.

Holmes, Urban T. *Spirituality for Ministry*. San Francisco: Harper & Row, 1982.

Horton, Michael. *Rediscovering the Holy Spirit*. Grand Rapids, MI: Zondervan, 2017.

Kellum, Nako. "The Importance of the Creeds in the Intersections of Our Lives." *Wesleyan Covenant*, February 5, 2019. https://wesleyancovenant.org/2019/02/04/the-importance-of-the-creeds-in-the-intersections-of-our-lives/.

LaSor, William S. *Men Who Knew Christ*. Glendale, CA: G/L Regal, 1971.

Lewis, C. S. *The Great Divorce*. New York: Macmillan, 1946.

———. *Letters to Malcolm: Chiefly on Prayer*. New York: Harvest, 1963.

Marty, Peter W. "Who Is Welcome at the Communion Table?" *The Christian Century*, October 10, 2021. https://www.christiancentury.org/article/editorpublisher/who-welcome-communion-table.

Miles, Sara. *Take This Bread: A Radical Conversion*. New York: Random House, 2008.

"Ministry." *Encyclopedia Britannica*, January 4, 2007. https://www.britannica.com/topic/ministry-Christianity.

Nettles, Thomas J. "History and Theories of Atonement." *The Gospel Coalition*, n.d. https://www.thegospelcoalition.org/essay/history-theories-atonement.

Okholm, Dennis. *Monk Habits for Everyday People*. Grand Rapids, MI: Brazos, 2007.

Orledge, Robert. *Gabriel Fauré*. London: Eulenburg, 1979.

"Our Story." https://www.sydneyoperahouse.com/our-story/sydney-opera-house-history.html.

Pruitt, Sarah. "Who Wrote the Bible?" *History*, July 17, 2020. https://www.history.com/news/who-wrote-the-bible.

Reeves, Ryan. "Did Luther Really Tell Us to 'Love God and Sin Boldly'?" *The Gospel Coalition*, n.d. https://www.thegospelcoalition.org/article/did-luther-really-tell-us-to-love-god-and-sin-boldly/.

Riches, John. *The Bible: A Very Short Introduction*. Oxford: Oxford University Press, 2000.

Rohr, Richard. *Falling Upward: A Spirituality for the Two Halves of Life*. San Francisco: Jossey-Bass, 2011.

———. *Things Hidden: Scripture as Spirituality*. Franciscan Media: 2007.

Schweitzer, Albert. *The Quest of the Historical Jesus: A Critical Study of its Progress from Reimarus to Wrede*. Translated by W. Montgomery. London: Black, 1911.

Severance, Cristin. "Unvaccinated Legacy Workers Face Termination after Religious Exemption Requests Denied." *KGW8*, October 30, 2021. https://www.kgw.com/article/news/health/coronavirus/vaccine/legacy-vaccine-religious-exemption-denied/283-1f64136c-5524-4f37-8432-5c95c45e61f9.

Smith, Huston. *The Soul of Christianity*. San Francisco: HarperCollins, 2005.

Snowden, James H. "The Place of Doubt in Religious Belief." *The Biblical World*. 47 (1916) 151–55. https://www.jstor.org/stable/3142911?seq=1#metadata_info_tab_contents.

Steinke, Peter L. *How Your Church Family Works*. Herndon, VA: Alban Institute, 1993.

Swan, Laura. *Engaging Benedict: What the Rule Can Teach Us Today*. Notre Dame, IN: Christian Classics, 2005.

Taylor, Barbara Brown. *An Altar in the World: A Geography of Faith*. New York: HarperCollins, 2009.

———. *Leaving Church: A Memoir of Faith*. San Francisco: HarperCollins, 2006.

"Theophilus of Antioch." https://en.wikipedia.org/wiki/Theophilus_of_Antioch.

Timpe, Kevin. "Sin in Christian Thought." *Stanford Encyclopedia of Philosophy*, 2021. https://plato.stanford.edu/entries/sin-christian/.

"Total Ministry." *An Episcopal Dictionary of the Church*.: Domestic and Foreign Missionary Society, 2021. https://www.episcopalchurch.org/glossary/total-ministry/.

Tutu, Desmond, ed. *An African Prayer Book*. New York: Image/Doubleday, 1995.

United Society. "Shore to Shore." In *Daily Prayers for All Seasons*, 122. New York: Church, 2014.

Van Oort, Johannes. "The Holy Spirit as Feminine: Early Christian Testimonies and Their Interpretation." *HTS Theological Studies* 72 (2016) 1–6. hts.org.za/index.php/hts/article/view/3225/7763.

Vest, Norvene. *Preferring Christ*. Trabuco Canyon, CA: Source, 1990.

Wakelee-Lynch, Julia, et al. *Daily Prayer for All Seasons*. New York: Church Publishing, 2014.

Warren, Tish Harrison. *Prayer in the Night*. Downers Grove, IL: InterVarsity, 2021.

Williams, Rowan. *Being Christian: Baptism, Bible, Eucharist, Prayer*. Grand Rapids, MI: Eerdmans, 2014.

Wright, N. T. "God." In *The Meaning of Jesus: Two Visions*, by Marcus Borg and N. T. Wright, 290–95. New York: HarperOne, 1999.

Zeitlin, Ariel. "24 Surprising Facts You Never Knew about the Bible." *Reader's Digest*, October 11, 2021. https://www.rd.com/list/bible-facts-you-never-knew.

Zizioulas, John. *Being as Communion: Studies in Personhood and the Church*. New York: St. Vladmir's Seminary, 1997.